MADHUR JAFFREY'S
SPICE KITCHEN

MADHUR JAFFREY'S SPICE KITCHEN

FIFTY RECIPES INTRODUCING INDIAN SPICES AND AROMATIC SEEDS

*Text and Drawings
by Madhur Jaffrey*

Culinary Alchemy™ Inc.
Contributing Editor

Carol Southern Books
New York

With my deepest appreciation —
For Elaine Markson and Carol Southern

Published by Carol Southern Books, 201 East 50th Street, New York, New York
10022. Member of the Crown Publishing Group.

Random House, Inc. New York, Toronto, London, Sydney, Auckland

. Carol Southern Books and Colophon are trademarks of Crown Publishers, Inc.

Manufactured in the United States

Contributing Editor: Culinary Alchemy™ Inc.

Design by Sharon Smith

Library of Congress Cataloging-in-Publication Data
Jaffrey, Madhur
[Spice kitchen]
Madhur Jaffrey's spice kitchen: fifty recipes introducing indian spices
and aromatic seeds / by Madhur Jaffrey — 1st ed.

p.   cm.
Includes Index.

1. Cookery, Indio. 2. Spices. I. Title
TX724.5.14J274   1993   93-25462
641.5954--dc20   CIP

ISBN 0-517-59698-9

10 9 8 7 6 5 4 3 2 1
First Edition

For
Zia, Meera, and Sakina

Other books by Madhur Jaffrey

Madhur Jaffrey's World-of-the-East
Vegetarian Cooking

An Invitation to Indian Cooking

Far Eastern Cookery

A Taste of India

Madhur Jaffrey's Menus for
Family and Friends

A Taste of the Far East

CONTENTS

THE WONDROUS PALETTE OF INDIAN SPICES & SEASONINGS

In painting, if you mix red and blue, they transform into purple. Blue and yellow magically turn into green. These are the ABCs of a painter's craft.

For over four thousand years Indians have been using spices as if they were colors on a vast palette: They have been added as accents; they have been juxtaposed; they have been put into a pot in quick succession so individual tastes could be experienced by diners in a cascade of varying sensations; and they have been combined to produce entirely new flavors. In short, spices have been used with a painterly mastery unique to Indian cuisine.

Some of the spices, like black pepper and cardamom, were indigenous to India. Others, like cumin, coriander, cloves, and cinnamon, arrived with traders, warriors, and immigrants in antiquity. The chilies of the New World came with Portuguese conquerors in the late fifteenth century. Whatever spices came into the country were analyzed and catalogued by our ancient system of *ayurvedic* medicine. Some "heated" the body (cinnamon), some "cooled" it (cumin), some aided digestion (asafetida), some were good for chest and throat ailments (ginger), and some acted as antiseptics (turmeric). The spices were then all added to the growing palette of "colors."

But each primary color has dozens of shades. Indians are masters at creating shades. Take cumin seeds. Their gentle, caraway-like flavor is just one shade of the spice. If whole seeds are dropped into hot oil and quickly fried, their taste and aroma is intensified and they turn quite nutty. On the other hand, if they are dry-roasted in a hot, cast-iron skillet and then ground, they turn earthy, musky, and exceedingly aromatic.

Or take mustard seeds. In the West, these seeds are associated with just one thing: sharpness and pungency. All Indians, however, know that mustard seeds, in reality, have a Jekyll-and-Hyde personality. If ground, they certainly are pungent and slightly bitter. However, if they are scattered in very hot oil first, they pop (literally) and turn very sweet and nutty.

What *is* all this about dropping or scattering whole spices in hot oil? It is the *tarka,* or "seasoning in oil," technique (known by many other names such as *baghaar* and *chhownk*), which is quite unique to India. Perhaps it is not all that unique in that it does exist, in the Mediterranean region — in very simple form.

In my early years in America, three decades ago, I — together with my then-boyfriend-now-husband — used to buy a lot of vegetables from Italian grocers in New York's Greenwich Village. Every time I saw a new vegetable, such as escarole or broccoli rabe, I wanted to try it. So I would ask the grocer how to cook it. His answer was always the same: "Take a little oil. Put in a little garlic, then put in . . . " (You have to say this with a heavy Italian accent to get it right.) Even today, when I am staring at a vegetable, wondering how to cook it, my husband starts in with, "Take a little oil . . . "

Well, an Indian might say that the Italian grocer was suggesting a *tarka* of garlic. When garlic pieces are scattered in hot oil and stirred around, their flavor intensifies. This flavor is quickly transferred to the oil. Everything cooked in that oil is then perfumed with garlic.

The same thing, and much more, happens with spices. First, the oil has to be so hot that the spices sizzle and pop instantly. Then, when spices are dropped into it, as with mustard seeds, their whole character can change. Since four or five spices can go into a *tarka,* they are often added to the hot oil in a certain order so those that burn easily, such as dried chilies, go in last. (In the case of the chilies, the flavor comes only from their browned skin.) The flavor of each spice is imparted to the oil. Any food cooked in this oil picks up the heightened flavor of all the spices.

Doing a *tarka* takes just a few seconds, so it is important to have all spices ready and at hand. A *tarka* is sometimes done at the beginning of a recipe and sometimes at the end. Legumes, for example, are usually just boiled with a little turmeric. When they are tender, a *tarka* is prepared in a small skillet, perhaps with asafetida, whole cumin, and red chilies, and then the entire contents of the skillet, hot oil and spices, are poured over the legumes with the lid shut tight for a few minutes to trap the aromas. These flavorings can be stirred in later. They perk up the boiled legumes and bring them to life. Sometimes *tarkas* are done twice, both at the beginning and end of a recipe.

Spices can be mixed and matched at will and once you know their properties and behavior, you can improvise freely. The purpose of this book is to show you how.

People often ask me why, since I am going to be mixing spices anyway, I do not use commercial curry powders. I always say that the genius of Indian cookery lies in mixing and matching different spices for each dish — some spices are used whole, some ground in water, some in vinegar, some dry-roasted. We know which spices can be overpowering and must be used in very small quantities (fenugreek, asafetida, *kalonji*) and which can be used more generously (coriander).

Sometimes we use just one spice in a dish, sometimes two, and sometimes fifteen. Sometimes we use the same spice twice in different ways. When preparing the sauce for a meat dish, we might first sauté a mixture of ground onions, garlic, and ginger — what I call the "wet trinity" — until brown. It gives the sauce its body. Then we add some ground cumin, coriander, and turmeric — what I call the "dry trinity." These need to be sautéed as well, as their raw taste is unpleasant. At a meal we like to have dishes that look and taste different from each other.

Of course, there are regional variations in the use of spices as well. In Bengal, for example, a popular *tarka* is done in mustard oil with *panchphoran,* a combination of whole spices — cumin, mustard, fenugreek, fennel, and *kalonji*. It gives foods a unique, anise-like flavor — a Bengali flavor.

If we are throwing a banquet and we wish to impress, we might cook a rice dish with expensive, aromatic saffron. For an everyday rice dish we might use the cheaper turmeric to color it, or just leave it plain. To cook with the same curry powder every day would render our rich and varied cuisine meaningless. It would be like asking to see a good painting and being shown the same Jackson Pollock each time. I want to sense the variety — see the Picassos, the Rembrandts, the da Vincis, the Mary Cassatts, and maybe a different painting by Pollock. With the correct use of spices, I can have that grand variety. And so can you.

In India, spices are generally ground on a grinding stone though many people have started using coffee grinders for dry spices and blenders for wet ones. I would suggest that you do the same. For very small quantities, a mortar and pestle is the best bet. To store spices, keep them in tightly closed containers in a dark cupboard. Spices stay fresh if they are left whole, but small quantities may be kept ground and used as needed.

How do you start? Plunge in. Choose any recipe in the book and follow it through. You will be painting with spices without even knowing it, experiencing four-thousand-year-old Indian traditions without leaving home.

Cinnamon

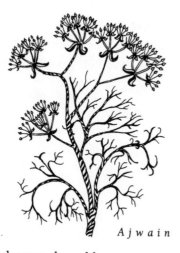

A j w a i n

AJWAIN (*or Ajwon*)

These small seeds look like celery seeds but taste more like a pungent version of thyme. (A student of mine compared *ajwain* to a mixture of anise and black pepper!) Used sparingly, as their flavor is strong, they are sprinkled into Indian breads, savory biscuits, and numerous noodlelike snacks made with chickpea flour. They also add a pleasant thymelike taste to vegetables such as green beans and potatoes and to roasted meats.

AMCHOOR (*Green Mango Powder*)

Unripe green mangoes are peeled, sliced, and their sour flesh sun-dried and ground to make *amchoor* powder. (The dried slices are also used in Indian cookery but not needed for recipes here.) The beige, slightly fibrous powder, rich in vitamin C, is tart but with a hint of sweetness and is used as lemon juice might be. It is particularly useful when sourness is required but the ingredients need to be kept dry, such as when sautéing spiced potatoes. As the powder can get

A m c h o o r

Asafetida

lumpy, crumble it well before using.

ASAFETIDA

The sap from the roots and stem of a giant fennel-like plant dries into a hard resin. It is sold in both lump and ground form. Only the ground form is used here. It has a strong, fetid aroma and is used in very small quantities both for its legendary digestive properties and for the much gentler, garliclike aroma it leaves behind after cooking. (James Beard compared it to the smell of truffles.) Asafetida is excellent with dried beans and vegetables. Store it in a tightly closed container.

BAY LEAVES

These dried leaves are added to many Indian rice and meat dishes for their delicate aroma. Sometimes they are lightly browned in oil first to intensify this aroma, using the *tarka* technique (page 10).

BLACK PEPPER

Native to India, whole peppercorns are added to rice and meat dishes for a mild peppery-lemony flavor. Ground pepper was once used in large amounts, sometimes as much

Bay Leaves

as several tablespoons in a single dish, especially in southern India where it grows. The arrival of the chili pepper from the New World around 1498 changed that usage somewhat though it still exists. In some southern Indian dishes, peppercorns are lightly roasted before use to draw out their lemony taste.

Black Pepper

CARDAMOM PODS AND SEEDS

Small green pods, the fruit of a gingerlike plant, hold clusters of black, highly aromatic seeds smelling like a combination of camphor, eucalyptus, orange peel, and lemon. Whole pods are put into rice and meat dishes and ground seeds are the main flavor in *garam masala* (page 20). This versatile spice is the vanilla of India and used in most desserts and sweetmeats. It is also added to spiced tea and sucked as a mouth freshener. Cardamom seeds that have been taken out of their pods are sold separately by Indian grocers. If you cannot get them, take the seeds out of the pods yourself. The most aromatic pods are green in color. The white pods sold by supermarkets have been bleached and have less flavor.

CAYENNE PEPPER

This is the hot powder that is made today by grinding the dried, red skins of several types of chili peppers. In India, and in Indian groceries here, it is simply called chili powder. But since that name can be confused with the Mexican-style chili powder that also contains cumin, garlic, and oregano, I am using the name "cayenne pepper" in all recipes. Even though chilies came from the New World, India today is the largest producer and one of the largest exporters and consumers. When adding to recipes, use your discretion. Cayenne pepper and India chili powder are sometimes available "hot" as well as regular. As "hot" can be too fiery and hard to control, it is best to get the regular kind.

CHILIES (Whole, Dried, Hot Red)

When whole, dried chilies are added to Indian food, it is generally done through the *tarka* method (page 10). A quick contact with very hot oil enhances and intensifies the flavor of their skins. It is that flavor Indians want. (Mexicans traditionally do this by roasting their chilies.)

Chilies

Then, if actual chili heat is desired, the chilies are allowed to stew with the food being cooked. The most commonly used dry chili is a cayenne type which is always slim but can vary in length from 1 to 4 inches. Its heat can also vary. Buy any that you can get easily.

Cinnamon

CINNAMON

Used mainly for desserts in the West, cinnamon, often in its "stick" form, is added to many Indian rice and meat dishes for its warm, sweet aroma. This inner bark from a laurel-like tree is also an important ingredient in the aromatic mixture *garam masala* (page 20).

CLOVES

Indians rarely use cloves in desserts, but they do use them in

meat and rice dishes and in the spice mixture *garam masala*. They carry pungently aromatic cloves, as well as cardamom pods, in tiny silver boxes to use as mouth fresheners when needed. For the same reason cloves are always part of the betel leaf paraphernalia that is offered as a digestive at the end of a meal.

CORIANDER SEEDS

Cloves

These ridged, beige seeds are sweetly spicy and cheap. As a result they are very commonly used in a great deal of Indian cookery. They are often the major part of many spice mixtures. In Maharashtra (western India), they are combined with cumin, shredded coconut, and other spices, then dry-roasted and ground to make a delicious black *masala* that is used with both meat and vegetables. In the southern state of Kerala, they are combined with

fenugreek seeds, black peppercorns, and red chilies, dry-roasted, and used to flavor shrimp and lobster dishes. In the North, coriander, cumin, and turmeric are a common trinity used in hundreds of dishes (see "dry trinity," page 12). For roasted ground cumin-coriander seeds, see Cumin.

CUMIN SEEDS

These look like caraway seeds but are slightly larger, plumper, and lighter in color. Their flavor is similar to caraway, only gentler

Cumin

and sweeter. They are used both whole and ground. When whole, they are often subjected to the *tarka* technique, page 10, which intensifies their flavor and makes them taste slightly nutty. When ground, they are used in meat, rice, and vegetable dishes. Cumin seeds can also be dry-roasted first and then ground. This version is sprinkled over many snack foods, relishes, and yogurt dishes. To dry-roast, put 3 to 4 tablespoons of whole cumin seeds into a heated, small cast-iron skillet. Keep over medium heat. Stir the cumin until it is a few shades darker and emits a distinct roasted aroma. Grind in a clean coffee grinder and store in a tightly lidded jar. In the west Indian state of Gujarat, cumin and coriander seeds are often dry-roasted together and then ground. To do this, combine 1 tablespoon each of cumin and coriander seeds in a heated, small cast-iron skillet set over a medium heat. Stir and roast until the spices turn a shade darker and emit a roasted aroma. Grind in a clean coffee grinder and store in a tightly lidded jar.

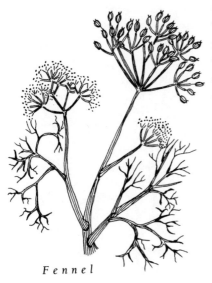

Fennel

CUMIN SEEDS (Black)

These are a rare, and therefore more expensive, form of cumin with sweeter, smaller, and more delicate seeds. Their mild pungency is perfect for the aromatic mixture of spices known as *garam masala* (page 20). The seeds can also be lightly dry-roasted and sprinkled whole over rice pilafs.

FENNEL SEEDS

These look a bit like cumin seeds but are much plumper and greener. Their flavor is decidedly anise-like. In Kashmir they are often ground and used in conjunction with asafetida and powdered ginger for a host of fish and vegetable dishes. In northern and western India, the whole seeds are used in pickles, chutneys, and snack foods. Using the *tarka* technique, they are also used in the stir-frying of vegetables, particularly in Bengal (eastern India), where they are part of the five-spice mixture called *panchphoran* (page 12). Fennel seeds can be dry-roasted and then eaten after a meal as both a digestive and mouth freshener.

Fenugreek

FENUGREEK SEEDS

It is these angular, yellowish seeds that give many commercial curry powders their earthy, musky "curry" aroma. In most of northern India they are used mainly in pickles, chutneys, and vegetarian dishes. In western, southern, and eastern India, they are used in meat and fish dishes as well (such as the *vindaloo* from Goa). They are a part of the Bengali spice mixture, *panchphoran*. Some Muslim communities in western India soak them to make a somewhat bitter but very cooling summer drink.

GARAM MASALA

This spice combination varies with each household, though the name is constant. *Garam* means "hot" and *masala* means "spices," so the spices in this mixture were traditionally those which "heated" the body according to the ancient *ayurvedic* system of medicine. It is important to note that the spices were not "chili-hot." The "heat" it implied was very similar to the *Yang* of China. The *Yin* and *Yang* theory of "cooling" and "heating" foods as well as *ayurvedic* medicine in India were probably, in their turn, influenced by the humoral theory of ancient Greece.

The *garam masala* spices not only "heated" the body, they all happened to be highly aromatic as well. Commercial mixtures tend to cut down on the expensive cardamom, the most aromatic of them all, and fill up with the cheaper coriander and cumin.

Here is how you make a classic ground mixture of *garam masala*: Combine in a clean coffee grinder 1 tablespoon cardamom seeds, 1 teaspoon whole cloves, 1 teaspoon whole black peppercorns, 1 teaspoon whole black cumin seeds, a 2-inch stick of cinnamon, 1/3 of a whole nutmeg, and a curl of mace. Grind until you have a fine powder. Store in a tightly closed jar and use as needed. Many people add a bay leaf to the mixture.

Generally, though not always, *garam masala* is sprinkled in towards the end of the cooking time to retain its aroma. The *garam masala* spices can also be used whole. If two or more of them are used together, they are still loosely referred to as *garam masala* as, even individually, they still have their "heating" properties.

Kalonji

KALONJI (Nigella)

Most Indians associate these black, teardrop-shaped seeds with *tandoor* oven breads (they are sprinkled over the top), pickles, Bengali food, including the Bengali five-spice mixture, *panchphoran,* and certain northern Indian vegetarian dishes. Their oreganolike taste is quite strong, so *kalonji* seeds should be used with some discretion.

MACE, see Nutmeg

MUSTARD SEEDS (Brown)

Of the three varieties of mustard seeds, white (actually yellow-

Mustard

ish), brown (a reddish-brown), and black (slightly larger, brownish black seeds), it is the brown that has been grown and used in India since antiquity. To confuse matters, the brown seeds are often referred to as black. When shopping, look for the small, reddish-brown variety although, in a pinch, any will do. The seeds have no aroma in their natural state and need to have something done to them to release both aroma and taste.

All mustard seeds have Jekyll-and-Hyde characteristics. When crushed, they are nose-tinglingly pungent. If they are thrown into hot oil and allowed to pop using the *tarka* method (page 10), however, they turn quite nutty and sweet, acquiring an earthy aroma in the bargain. In India, both these techniques are used, sometimes in the same recipe. Whole mustard seeds, popped in oil, are used to season vegetables, legumes, yogurt relishes, salads, and rice dishes. Crushed seeds are used to steam fish, in sauces, and in pickles.

NUTMEG AND MACE

Nutmegs are the dried seeds of a round pearlike fruit. Mace is the red lacy covering around the seeds that turns yellowish when dried. Both have similar warm, sweetish, and slightly cam-

Nutmeg

phorous flavors, though mace has a slightly bitter edge. Both nutmeg and mace are used here in the *garam masala* mixture (page 20). A nutmeg breaks easily. Just hit it lightly with a hammer to get the third needed for the *garam masala* recipe. Indians almost never use nutmeg for desserts and drinks.

RAI MASALA

Rai is the Indian name for the mustard seeds that give this spice mixture its pungency and name. All spices are lightly roasted before being ground. To make *rai masala,* put 2 tablespoons whole coriander seeds, 1 teaspoon whole cumin seeds, 1 teaspoon whole fenugreek seeds, 1 teaspoon whole brown mustard seeds, 1 teaspoon whole peppercorns, 1 to 2 dried, hot, red chilies, and 5 whole cloves into a heated, medium-sized cast-iron skillet and set over medium heat. Stir and dry-roast until some of the spices turn a shade darker and just begin to emit a roasted aroma. Allow to cool slightly and then grind finely in a clean coffee grinder or other spice grinder. Store in a tightly closed container.

TAMARIND

The fruit of a tall shade tree, tamarinds look like wide beans. As they ripen, their sour green flesh turns a chocolate color. It remains sour but picks up a hint of sweetness. For commercial purposes, tamarinds are peeled, seeded, semi-dried, and their brown flesh compacted into rectangular blocks. These blocks are then broken up and soaked in water the pulp can be pushed through a strainer. This is tamarind paste. (See page 108 for

Tamarind

details.) The paste is a souring agent used for many legume, vegetable, and fish dishes. It is also made into chutneys.

TURMERIC

A rhizome like ginger, only with smaller, more delicate "fingers," fresh turmeric is quite orange inside. When dried, it turns bright yellow. It is this musky yellow powder that gives some Indian dishes a yellowish cast. As it is inexpensive and considered to be an antiseptic, turmeric is used freely in the cooking of legumes, vegetables, and meats.

Turmeric

Special Ingredients

BASMATI RICE

This is a very fine, long-grain, highly aromatic rice grown in the foothills of the Himalaya mountains. The better varieties are generally aged a year before being sold. This rice is now being grown in America as well, but, for my taste, does not yet have either the fine texture or the flowery aroma of Indian rice. The variety now grown in Texas is sold as Texmati. It may be used, in exactly the same way as basmati, as a second choice. Basmati grains are very delicate so stirring must be done very gently so as not to break the grain.

MIXED MUNG AND MASOOR DAL

A *dal* is a dried pea or bean that has been split though the name is now used more generally to include most dried peas and beans. Mung *dal* consists of hulled and split mung beans and is sold by all Indian and some Chinese grocers. *Masoor dal* is red lentils, sold by most health food stores under that name. The two *dals* can, of course, be cooked separately. I often combine them, either in equal quantities or 2/3 mung and 1/3 *masoor*, for a wonderful, earthy taste. The grains of red lentils sold by health food stores tend to be larger and prettier, but have less flavor and are much more dry and floury than the smaller ones sold by Indian grocers. All red lentils turn yellow after cooking.

URAD DAL

A small, pale yellow split pea that is used, among other things, to make all manner of South Indian pancakes. In this book, however, it is used only as a seasoning. It is South Indians who seem to have discovered that if you throw a few of these dried split peas into hot oil, using the *tarka* method, the seeds will turn red and acquire the taste of roasted peanuts. Anything stir-fried in the oil afterwards will pick up that nutty flavor and aroma.

Fresh Seasonings

GARLIC

Some Indians (Kashmiri Hindus, the Jain sect) do not touch garlic but the rest of the country eats it with pleasure. It is an important ingredient in meat sauces, which often require that onion, garlic, and ginger — the "wet trinity" of seasonings — be ground into a paste and then fried in oil until dark and thick. In parts of Saurashtra (western India), garlic, salt, and dried red chilies are pounded together to make an everyday condiment.

GINGER

The pungent fresh rhizome is ground and used in meat sauces (see Garlic) and in drinks. It is also cut into slivers or minute dice and used when stir-frying potatoes, green beans, spinach, and other vegetables. Store ginger in the refrigerator but keep it dry or it will spoil. For Indian recipes, ginger is always peeled first, something the Chinese do not always require.

GREEN CHILIES

The fresh green chili used in India cooking is of the cayenne type, generally about 3 inches long and slender but sometimes smaller. I refer to this as a "fresh, long, hot green chile." Its heat can vary from mild to fiery. (Bees, it seems, unthinkingly cross-pollinate different varieties that grow in proximity.) The only way to judge the heat is by tasting a tiny piece of skin from the middle section. (Keep some yogurt handy!) The top part of the chili with more seeds is always the hottest; the bottom tip, the mildest. The hot seeds of the chili are never removed in India but you may do so if you wish.

Use whatever chili you can find. The most commonly available one in the United States is the jalapeño, which is thicker skinned and hotter than the Indian chili. The smaller Thai "bird's eye" chili, also a cayenne variety, may also be substituted. It is fiery. Use both with discretion. Also wash hands well after handling chilies. If you touch your eyes, mouth, or nose without washing your hands first, they may burn.

GREEN CORIANDER (Chinese Parsley, Cilantro)

The green leaves of the coriander plant are India's favorite herb. They are ground into fresh chutneys, mixed in with vegetables, cooked with chicken, and used as a garnish. When green coriander is called for, chop up the top of the plant where the stalks are slender. From the lower half, where the stalks are thicker, you will have to pick off the leaves. To store, stand the coriander stalks, roots and all, in a glass of water with the leafy part above the water level. Pull a plastic bag over the whole thing and refrigerate.

ONIONS

Onions are used routinely for meat sauces (see Garlic) and for flavoring rice, vegetable, and legume dishes. One uncommon usage is to fry very thin slices until they turn crisp and brown and then to use them as a garnish or incorporate them into, say, a dish of sautéed okra.

SOUPS AND APPETIZERS

SOOTHING CAULIFLOWER SOUP WITH CORIANDER

Gobi Ka Shorva

If there is a trinity of the most commonly used dry spices, it is surely ground cumin, ground coriander, and turmeric. Often they are used together and some kind of ground chilies are invariably added to the threesome to provide heat. As they are powdery and can burn easily, it is a good idea to have them all measured into a small bowl before you start. They go into the pot together and cook very briefly, with just a quick stir to take away their raw taste. Keep the ingredients that follow at hand to prevent burning.

This dish also contains the favored Indian trinity of fresh seasonings: onion, garlic, and ginger. In this recipe ginger predominates, adding a pungent freshness.

This soup may be served as an elegant first course at a grand dinner or as part of a simple lunch, accompanied, perhaps, by a sandwich or salad or both. It may be made a day in advance and refrigerated. Reheat over fairly low heat.

SERVES 4 TO 6

3 tablespoons vegetable oil

2 medium onions, peeled and chopped

A 1-inch piece of fresh ginger, peeled and cut into fine slivers

4 garlic cloves, peeled and chopped

1 teaspoon ground cumin

2 teaspoons ground coriander

1/4 teaspoon turmeric

1/8 – 1/4 teaspoon cayenne pepper

1/2 pound potatoes (2 medium), peeled and cut into rough 1/2-inch dice

1/2 pound (2 heaping cups) cauliflower flowerets

7 cups chicken stock, fresh or canned

Salt, if needed
1 cup heavy cream

Heat the oil over fairly high heat in a large pot. When hot, put in the onions, ginger, and garlic. Stir-fry for about 4 minutes, or until the onions are somewhat browned. Add the cumin, coriander, turmeric, and cayenne. Stir once and add the potatoes, cauliflower, and chicken stock. If the stock is unsalted, add 3/4 teaspoon salt. Stir and bring to a boil. Cover, turn heat to low, and simmer gently for 10 minutes, or until potatoes are tender. Taste for salt, adding more if you like.

Put the soup into a blender, in 2 or more batches as required, and blend thoroughly. Strain, pushing down to get all the pulp. Add the cream and mix. The soup may now be reheated and served.

Turmeric

YOGURT SOUP WITH CUMIN
Safed Shorva

For North Indians, the creamy tartness of yogurt and the earthy nuttiness of cumin seeds, which have been roasted and ground, go together like — well — a horse and carriage. Cumin is also considered to be a cooling spice, so this light, delightful cold soup is perfect for a warm summer day. It is very gently spiced, as a lot of Indian dishes are. And it needs no cooking! I use low-fat yogurt, but you could just as easily use the creamier full-fat variety.

If you are in a hurry, you can just chop up the tomato, but it is preferable to peel and seed it first. I use one large tomato and simply drop it into boiling water for 15 seconds and then peel it. Then, I cut it in half crosswise, gently squeeze out all the seeds, and dice the shell.

Refrigerate the chicken stock, then strain it so that no particles of congealed fat fall into the soup.

SERVES 4

2 1/2 cups plain yogurt

3 3/4 cups chicken stock, fresh or canned, all fat removed

1/2 teaspoon peeled fresh ginger, grated very finely to a pulp

1/2 cup peeled, seeded, and finely diced cucumber

1/2 cup finely diced, peeled, and seeded tomato (see above)

1/8 teaspoon cayenne pepper

1/2 teaspoon ground roasted cumin seeds (page 18)

2 teaspoons finely chopped fresh mint or green coriander
    (Chinese parsley, cilantro), or a mixture of the two

Freshly ground black pepper to taste

Put the yogurt in a bowl. Beat with a fork until smooth and creamy. Slowly add the stock, mixing it in as you do so. Add all the remaining ingredients and mix. Refrigerate until needed. Stir well before serving.

SPICY CASHEWS

Tale Caju

Cashews that have been freshly fried at home have an exquisite taste, far better than that of the canned or bottled varieties. In India, this was the only kind of cashew we ate; my mother fried the nuts just before my father sat down for his evening Scotch and soda. The spices here are typical of many North Indian snacks — salt, pepper, cayenne, and the wonderfully aromatic roasted cumin.

Raw cashews can be bought at most health food stores.

SERVES 4 TO 6

Vegetable oil for deep-frying
2 cups raw cashew nuts
1/4 teaspoon salt
Freshly ground black pepper
1/4 teaspoon cayenne pepper
1/2 teaspoon ground roasted cumin seeds (page 18)

Put a sieve on top of a metal bowl and set it near the stove. Line 2 plates with paper towels and set them nearby.

Heat about 1 inch of oil in a deep 8-inch frying pan over medium heat. When hot, put in all the cashews. Stir-fry them until they turn reddish gold. This happens fairly fast. Empty the contents of the frying pan into the sieve to drain the oil. Lift up the sieve and shake out all the extra oil. Spread the cashews out on one of the plates and sprinkle the salt, pepper, cayenne, and cumin on them. Mix well. Slide the cashews on to the second plate; this will take some more of the oil off them. Serve cashews warm or after they have cooled.

Note: The oil used for frying may be reused.

AJWAIN-FLAVORED CHICKEN
Murgh Ke Mazedar Tukray

Ajwain seeds, which look and taste a bit like celery seeds, are always used sparingly as their taste is quite assertive. In India, they are used with roasted meats, some breads, and a host of munchable snacks.

The spice mixture used here, which has a lot of black pepper in it, is also excellent on broiled fish, steaks, and chops.

These spicy chicken cubes may be served hot, warm, or cold. They may be pierced with toothpicks and nibbled on with drinks, added to salads, or eaten at picnics. They may also be served as a main course with rice or potatoes and a green salad.

SERVES 6 TO 8 AS AN APPETIZER,
4 AS A MAIN COURSE

1 1/4 pounds boneless and skinless chicken breasts (4 breast
  halves)

1 teaspoon freshly ground black pepper

1/4 teaspoon turmeric

1/4 teaspoon or more cayenne pepper

1 teaspoon ground cumin

1/2 teaspoon ajwain seeds

3/4 teaspoon salt

1 garlic clove, peeled and crushed to a pulp

About 3 tablespoons vegetable oil

Preheat the oven to 350° F.

Cut each chicken piece into thirds lengthwise, and then crosswise into 3/4- to 1-inch segments. Put in a bowl and add the black pepper, turmeric, cayenne, cumin, *ajwain*, salt, garlic, and 1 tablespoon of the oil. Mix well and set aside for 15 to 30 minutes or longer, covering and refrigerating if necessary.

Heat the remaining 2 tablespoons oil in a wok or large non-stick frying pan over very high heat. When very hot, put in the chicken. Stir-fry until chicken pieces are lightly browned or turn opaque on the outside. Put in a baking dish and cover loosely with lightly oiled wax paper. The wax paper should be inside the dish and directly on the chicken pieces. Bake for 8 to 10 minutes, or until the chicken pieces are just cooked through. If not eating immediately, remove the chicken pieces from the baking dish to prevent them from drying out.

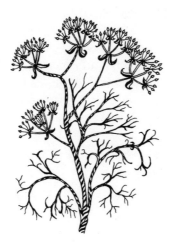

A j w a i n

EASY KEBABS

Tala Gosht

In this recipe, a marinade of dry spices and fresh seasonings flavors and tenderizes the lamb. The dry spices are the highly aromatic ones in the mixture *garam masala* — black pepper, cardamom, cloves, nutmeg, black cumin, and cinnamon. It is added near the end of the cooking so its aroma stays strong.

Of the fresh seasonings, ginger does double duty, adding pungency and tenderizing. Fresh green chilies provide much of the heat, but a different heat from dried red chilies, as the flavors of their skins are completely different. The green skins are fresh and herblike whereas the dried ones are muskier.

This dish cooks in about 15 minutes, but needs to be marinated for 2 hours. The kebabs make a wonderful cocktail snack — just stick toothpicks into the meat pieces. Or, serve them as an entrée with Indian bread or rice, a legume such as the Lentils with Cumin and Asafetida on page 59, a green vegetable such as spinach (page 54), and a yogurt relish.

SERVES 6

2 pounds boneless lamb meat from the shoulder, cut into
*   1 1/4 – 1 1/2-inch cubes*

4 teaspoons peeled fresh ginger, grated very finely to a pulp

2 teaspoons very finely crushed garlic

4 fresh long hot green chilies or 1 jalapeño, finely minced

1/2 teaspoon cayenne pepper

1 1/2 teaspoons salt

Freshly ground black pepper

2 tablespoons vegetable oil

1 teaspoon ground garam masala *(page 20)*

Mint sprigs and wedges of lime or lemon

Cut each cube of meat into narrower 1/4-inch-thick pieces. Pound the pieces with a meat mallet or potato masher so they flatten out slightly.

Combine the ginger, garlic, green chilies, cayenne, and salt and rub into the meat. Grind lots of black pepper over the meat and rub that in as well. Set the meat aside for 2 hours or longer, covering and refrigerating, if necessary.

Heat the oil in a large nonstick frying pan over medium-low heat. Put in all the meat and slowly bring to a simmer. Cover and continue to cook over medium-low heat for about 15 minutes, or until the meat is tender. The meat will cook in its own juices.

Remove the cover and turn up the heat a bit. Add the *garam masala*. Boil away all the liquid and gently fry the meat so it turns slightly brown. Serve with mint sprigs and lime or lemon wedges.

Chilies

A DRY CHUTNEY OR "DIP"

Sookhi Chutney

Not all chutneys are wet or sweet or, for that matter, meant to be eaten with meals. This dry, savory one is a wonderful dip for raw vegetables. It consists mainly of cumin and coriander seeds that have been roasted and ground, turning them quite nutty. Roasted almonds are added to the mix to enhance the nutty flavor.

Arrange all the vegetables, such as cauliflower flowerets, green beans, cucumber sticks, carrot sticks, and radishes, around a bowl of the dip and serve with drinks. I usually put a bowl of water (or gin!) near the vegetables so they can be moistened slightly before being dipped into the spice mixture. This helps the spices to adhere to the vegetables.

This spice mixture may be frozen.

MAKES 1 CUP

2 tablespoons coriander seeds

1 tablespoon cumin seeds

3 tablespoons blanched slivered almonds

2 tablespoons coarse salt

1/4 teaspoon cayenne pepper, or more to taste

1/4 teaspoon freshly ground black pepper

Put the coriander seeds, cumin seeds, and almonds into a small, heavy skillet over medium-low heat. Dry-roast, stirring gently until the seeds and nuts are a few shades darker and emit a deliciously nutty odor. Empty the spices onto a plate and let them cool slightly. Put them in a clean coffee grinder and grind as finely as possible.

Place the spice mixture in a serving bowl. Add the salt, cayenne, and black pepper. Mix.

VEGETABLES, LEGUMES,
RICE, AND BREAD

TANGY GREEN BEANS WITH AJWAIN AND GINGER

Chatpatee Sem

Here, green beans are blanched so they become porous enough to absorb seasonings. Then they are stir-fried quickly in oil that has been flavored with a *tarka* (page 10) of *ajwain,* cumin seeds, ginger, and onion. As they are stirred, ground cumin, coriander, cayenne, and sour *amchoor* powder are sprinkled over the top. There is some more quick stirring to allow the spices to "cook." Then, to make the dry spices adhere to the beans, a tablespoon or two of water is sprinkled in as well. All this happens very quickly indeed, so it helps to have the seasonings measured and ready near the stove. Incidentally, this combination of spices and techniques may be used for cooking sliced carrots, boiled diced potatoes, diced yellow squash, cauliflower flowerets, and fine fingers of peeled kohlrabi.

These green beans may be served with a rice dish, almost any meat dish of your choice, and Lentils with Cumin and Asafetida (page 59) for a simple meal. Vegetarians might prefer to leave out the meat, adding instead another vegetable such as Eggplant Baked in a Sweet-and-Sour Tamarind Sauce (page 46) and a yogurt relish. For an elegant seafood dinner, serve the beans with Shrimp in a Creamy, Aromatic Sauce (page 72) and Rice and Peas with Garam Masala (page 65).

SERVES 4 TO 5

Salt

1 pound green beans, trimmed

4 tablespoons vegetable oil

1 teaspoon cumin seeds

1/4 teaspoon ajwain *seeds*

1/2 medium onion, peeled and cut into thin half-rings

A 3/4-inch piece of fresh ginger, peeled, very finely sliced, and cut into minute dice

1 teaspoon ground cumin

1 teaspoon ground coriander

1/4 teaspoon cayenne pepper, or to taste

2 teaspoons well-crumbled amchoor powder

Bring 5 quarts of water to a rolling boil. Add 2 tablespoons salt. Stir and add the green beans. Boil rapidly for 4 to 5 minutes, or until the beans are cooked through. Drain.

Heat the oil in a wok, large frying pan, or wide pot over medium-high heat. When very hot, add the cumin and *ajwain* seeds. Stir for 10 seconds and add the onion. Lower the heat to medium, stir, and let the onion brown lightly. Add the ginger and stir for 20 seconds. Add the green beans and give a quick toss. Sprinkle in the ground cumin, coriander, cayenne, and 3/4 teaspoon salt. Toss once or twice. Put in the *amchoor* and 2 tablespoons water, toss to mix, and serve.

A m c h o o r

BROCCOLI WITH GARLIC AND MUSTARD SEEDS

Subzi

One of the very simple methods of cooking green vegetables in Bengal is to give a *tarka* (page 10) of mustard seeds using mustard oil (extra-virgin olive oil gives an equally intense, though different flavor) and then adding green chilies towards the end of the cooking, which lend the flavor of their skins as well.

This may be served with almost all beef, pork, lamb, chicken, or fish dishes in this book. Rice should be served on the side, along with a chutney or a yogurt relish.

SERVES 6

5 tablespoons mustard oil or extra-virgin olive oil

1 teaspoon brown mustard seeds

2 – 3 garlic cloves, peeled and finely minced

2 pounds broccoli, trimmed and cut into spears or broccoli rabe cut crosswise into wide ribbons

1/2 – 3/4 teaspoon salt

4 tablespoons chicken broth, homemade or canned

2 fresh long hot green chilies or 1/2 jalapeño, cut crosswise into 2 to 3 parts

Heat the oil in a wok or a large, wide pan over medium-high heat. When hot, put in the mustard seeds. As soon as the mustard seeds begin to pop — this takes just a few seconds — add the garlic. Stir once or twice, then put in the broccoli or broccoli rabe. Stir a few times and then add the salt and chicken broth. Stir and cover. Cook over medium heat for 2 minutes. Add the chilies and cook another minute or so for the broccoli and another 5 minutes over medium-low heat for the broccoli rabe. Remove cover, and if there is liquid left, turn the heat up to boil it away. Stir gently a few times as you do this.

CARROTS WITH RAISINS, AJWAIN, AND MINT

Pudina Gajar

The sweetness of the carrots in this recipe is enhanced by the golden raisins, complemented by the thymelike flavor of *ajwain* and the cool freshness of mint. A split pea, *urad dal*, is used here as a spice. It is given a *tarka* in oil and turns very nutty, offering the dish a taste akin to that of roasted peanuts. Serve this recipe with Western-style roast duck or broiled chicken, or with any lamb, pork, or beef dish in this book, along with a rice and perhaps Spinach with Ginger, Fennel, and Black Cumin (page 54).

SERVES 4

2 tablespoons vegetable oil

1/4 teaspoon ajwain seeds

1/4 teaspoon urad dal

1/2 medium onion, peeled and cut into thin half-rings

3 – 4 tablespoons golden raisins

1 pound carrots, peeled and cut into 1/4-inch-thick rounds

1 fresh long hot green chili, cut into thin rounds or 1/3 jalapeño, finely chopped

4 tablespoons finely chopped fresh mint

1/4 teaspoon salt, or to taste

1/4 teaspoon sugar

Heat the oil in a frying pan over medium-high heat. When very hot, put in the *ajwain* seeds and the *urad dal*. Stir once or twice. The *dal* will turn red. Stir once and put in the onion. Stir-fry until onion just starts to brown. Add the raisins. Stir once or twice. Add the carrots, green chili, and mint. Turn the heat down to medium and sauté for 1 minute. Put in the salt, sugar, and 2 tablespoons water. Stir once. Cover, lower heat, and cook for about 3 minutes, or until carrots are just tender.

BROWNED CABBAGE WITH FENNEL AND ONIONS

Bhuni Band Gobi

Even though there are cumin, fenugreek, and mustard seeds in this dish, the most assertive flavor is that of fennel, which is a strong spice. When combined with browned cabbage and onions, it becomes a heady mixture.

Spices are added here in three lots. The first group of whole seeds goes in at the beginning as a *tarka* (page 10). The second, of ground spices and seasonings, is first sautéed thoroughly and then mixed into the partly cooked cabbage. The aromatic *garam masala* goes in towards the end, so its perfume holds until the food is consumed.

Serve with any lamb or pork dish in this book or as part of a vegetarian meal with Lentils with Cumin and Asafetida (page 59), Griddle Breads with *Ajwain* and Black Pepper (page 66), Bazaar Potatoes (page 52), and a yogurt relish.

SERVES 4 TO 6

1 medium head green cabbage

2 1/2 medium onions

1/2 cup vegetable oil

5 fenugreek seeds

1/2 teaspoon cumin seeds

1/4 teaspoon brown mustard seeds

1/2 teaspoon fennel seeds

2 garlic cloves, peeled and coarsely chopped

A 1 1/2-inch piece of fresh ginger, peeled and coarsely chopped

1 medium canned or 1 ripe tomato, peeled and seeded and chopped

1/2 teaspoon turmeric

1 fresh long hot green chili or 1/3 to 1/2 jalapeño, thinly sliced

1 3/4 teaspoon salt

1 teaspoon ground garam masala (page 20)

1 tablespoon lemon juice

Trim away the outer damaged leaves of the cabbage, wash cabbage, and cut it into quarters. Core and shred cabbage lengthwise as thinly as possible.

Peel 2 of the onions and cut them in half lengthwise, then slice into thin half-circles.

Heat 5 tablespoons of the oil in a wide, heavy-bottomed pot over medium heat, and add the fenugreek, cumin, mustard, and fennel seeds. As the seeds start sizzling and changing color (about 10 seconds), put in the sliced onions. Fry over medium heat for about 3 minutes, then add the shredded cabbage. Stir a few times, put the lid on, lower heat, and cook for 15 minutes.

Uncover and cook over fairly low heat for 30 minutes more, stirring occasionally to prevent burning. The cabbage and onions will brown slightly.

Meanwhile, peel and coarsely chop the remaining 1/2 onion and put it with the garlic, ginger, and tomato in a blender. Blend to a paste.

In a skillet, heat the 3 remaining tablespoons of oil. Add the paste from the blender, turmeric, and chili. Fry, stirring all the time, for 8 to 10 minutes. If necessary, add 1 teaspoon warm water at a time to prevent sticking. When the cabbage has cooked for 30 minutes, add this fried paste to the pot, along with the salt, *garam masala,* and lemon juice. Stir and cook for another 5 minutes.

STIR-FRIED CAULIFLOWER
WITH GINGER

Sookhi Gobi

This cauliflower is gently spiced, with the flavor of fresh ginger predominating. The ginger and the asafetida have two functions: they add taste and they help make cauliflower more digestible. Again, there is *amchoor* to provide a hint of tartness and the *garam masala* to provide the final aroma.

This cauliflower can be served with almost all Indian meals. Try it with Peshawari Kebabs (page 96) or any lamb or pork dish. I find it also complements meals of roasted and broiled meats. I love to add leftovers, if there are any, cold and straight out of the refrigerator, to a dressed green salad – a final toss and it is ready to be eaten with cold meats or other salads.

SERVES 6

A 1-inch cube of fresh ginger, peeled

6 tablespoons vegetable oil

1/8 teaspoon ground asafetida

1/8 teaspoon cumin seeds

1/4-1/2 teaspoon cayenne pepper

4 teaspoons ground coriander

1/2 teaspoon turmeric

A 2-pound head of cauliflower, cut into small flowerets

1 1/2 teaspoons salt

1/2 teaspoon ground garam masala *(page 20)*

1 teaspoon ground amchoor

Cut the ginger crosswise into very thin slices. Stacking several of the slices over each other at a time, cut them first into very thin strips and then crosswise into minute dice.

Heat the oil in a very large frying pan, wok, or other wide utensil over medium-high heat. When hot, add the asafetida and, a second later, the cumin seeds. As soon as the cumin seeds begin to sizzle, add the ginger. Stir the ginger for a few seconds, until it just starts to brown. Now add the cayenne pepper, coriander, and turmeric. Stir once and quickly add the cauliflower and salt. Stir the cauliflower for 1 minute. Add 4 tablespoons water and cover the pan immediately. Turn heat to low and cook for 5 to 10 minutes, or until the cauliflower is just tender. Stir once or twice during this period. (Add 1 tablespoon more water if it seems to be going to dry out.)

When the cauliflower is just done, remove the lid. If there is any liquid in the pan, evaporate it by turning up the heat a bit. Sprinkle the *garam masala* and *amchoor* over the top and stir gently to mix.

A s a f e t i d a

EGGPLANT BAKED IN A SWEET-AND-SOUR TAMARIND SAUCE

Khatte Meethe Baigan

In this recipe, eggplants are grilled, brushed with a sweet-and-sour tamarind chutney, and baked; it is as simple as that. The tamarind chutney is the key here. The naturally tangy taste of tamarind combined with the nutty, musky aroma of roasted and ground cumin seeds is quite irresistible.

I use the slim, long, pinkish-mauve eggplants that are sometimes called Japanese eggplants. If you cannot find them, use the large oval ones. Just cut them crosswise into rounds.

Bake the eggplants in the same dish you serve them. I use an oval dish that is about 10 inches long and about 2 1/2 inches high, but you could just as easily use a square or rectangular dish.

Serve with Chicken and Peas with Cinnamon and Bay Leaves (page 78), Silken Chicken (page 80), or any lamb dish. Rice should be served on the side.

SERVES 6

2 1/2 pounds eggplants

6 – 8 tablespoons vegetable oil

Salt

Freshly ground black pepper

3 tablespoons Tamarind Chutney (page 108), diluted with
*   3 tablespoons water*

Preheat the broiler.

Cut the eggplants somewhat diagonally into 1/3-inch-thick oval slices. Brush generously on both sides with oil. Sprinkle each side lightly with salt and pepper as well. Put as many slices as will fit in a single layer in a broiling tray and cook on both sides until golden red. Repeat for remaining eggplants.

Preheat the oven to 350° F.

Arrange the eggplant slices in a baking dish in slightly over-lapping rows. When the bottom is covered with a layer of slices, drizzle a third of the chutney over them and spread it evenly with your fingers. Cover the first layer with 2 more layers of eggplant, coating each with the chutney. Cover the baking dish with foil and bake for 20 minutes.

Tamarind

PEAS WITH WHOLE CUMIN AND MUSTARD SEEDS

Malaidar Matar

The *tarka*, page 10, this time is of cumin and mustard seeds, but they provide only the background taste. It is the tomato-cream sauce, flavored with the aromatic *garam masala*, that provides for the main flavors in this fine dish.

This may be served with Delectable Pork in a Mustard Spice Mix (page 88) or Lamb in a Tomato Sauce (page 94). Griddle Breads with *Ajwain* and Black Pepper (page 66), store-bought whole wheat pita bread, or rice may be served on the side. It also goes well with Western lamb and pork roasts.

SERVES 5 TO 6

1/4 teaspoon sugar

1/2 teaspoon ground cumin

1/2 teaspoon ground garam masala (*page 20*)

3/4 teaspoon salt

1/4 – 1/2 teaspoon cayenne pepper

1 tablespoon tomato paste

3/4 cup heavy cream

1 tablespoon lemon juice

2 tablespoons chopped green coriander (Chinese parsley, cilantro)

1 fresh long hot green chili or 1/3 jalapeño, finely chopped

4 cups shelled fresh peas or frozen, defrosted under warm water and drained

3 tablespoons vegetable oil

1/2 teaspoon cumin seeds

1/2 teaspoon brown mustard seeds

Combine the sugar, ground cumin, *garam masala,* salt, cayenne pepper, and tomato paste. Slowly add 2 tablespoons water, mixing as you go. Add the cream slowly and mix. Put in the lemon juice, green coriander, and chili. Mix again and set aside.

If the peas are fresh, drop them into 4 cups of boiling water and cook until just barely done. Drain.

Heat the oil in a large frying pan over medium-high heat. When hot, put in the cumin and mustard seeds. As soon as the mustard seeds begin to pop (this just takes a few seconds), add the peas. Stir and sauté for 30 seconds. Add the cream sauce. Cook over high heat for about 1 1/2 minutes, or until the sauce has thickened, stirring gently as you do so.

M u s t a r d

SPICY, SOUR POTATOES WITH CUMIN AND AMCHOOR

Khatte Zeera Aloo

These potatoes, which can be served with both Eastern and Western meals, get their main flavoring from cumin, both whole and ground. The tartness comes from *amchoor*, the sour mango powder, and from lemon juice. The complex taste, which also includes the pungency of fresh ginger, is what Indians would describe as *chatpatah*, which implies a finger-licking, hot-sour quality associated with spicy street snacks.

Once the potatoes have boiled, this dish cooks fast, so have everything measured, ready, and at hand.

Serve with Delectable Pork in a Mustard Spice Mix (page 88) or with Barbecued Leg of Lamb with a Spicy, Lemony Marinade (page 100), along with Spinach with Ginger, Fennel, and Black Cumin (page 54) or as part of a vegetarian meal with vegetables, yogurt dishes, rice, and Lentils with Cumin and Asafetida (page 59).

SERVES 6

1 3/4 pounds (about 4 large) waxy boiling potatoes, such as
   Maine Eastern potatoes

4 tablespoons vegetable oil

A generous pinch of ground asafetida

1 teaspoon cumin seeds

1/4 teaspoon ajwain seeds

A 1-inch piece of fresh ginger, peeled, thinly sliced, and then cut
   into minute dice

1 tablespoon ground cumin

1 1/2 teaspoons ground amchoor, well crumbled

1/4 teaspoon cayenne pepper, or to taste

1 tablespoon lemon juice

1 teaspoon salt, or to taste

Freshly ground black pepper

2 tablespoons chopped leaves of green coriander (Chinese parsley, cilantro), optional

Boil the potatoes. Allow them to cool, then peel and cut them into 1/2-inch dice.

Heat the oil in a large nonstick frying pan over medium-high heat. When hot, add first the asafetida, then the cumin and *ajwain*. Ten seconds later, put in the ginger. Stir once or twice, then add the potatoes, ground cumin, *amchoor*, cayenne, lemon juice, salt, and pepper. Stir to mix thoroughly and heat through. Add the coriander and mix again.

A m c h o o r

BAZAAR POTATOES
Bazaari Aloo

It is quite possible that because food from the small stalls and tiny restaurants in the bazaars of Delhi, my hometown, were forbidden to us as children, we acquired a wild love for them. But those foods did have, and still have, a fire and passion that the more classic cooking in our home never even aimed for. They also had, and still have, a very special taste. That taste did not come from the sweat of "unclean" workers, as my finicky father used to say, but rather from very special combinations of seasonings. In the Delhi of my childhood, the vegetarian stalls almost never used onion and garlic, which, I learned much later in life, were meant to arouse the "baser passions." Ginger, it seems, kept the inner soul on an even keel so it alone was used among the "wet" seasonings.

But there has been an evolution in the use of seasonings, just as in fashion. After Indian independence in 1947, there was an enormous influx of refugees from the part of Punjab that had now become Pakistan, and with the Punjabis — who more than quadrupled Delhi's population overnight — came a new brand of bazaar vegetable cooking that used onions and garlic freely and that also added tomatoes — something the old Delhi bazaar shops had done only with some reluctance. Here is a contemporary bazaar recipe that has bits of the old — the asafetida, cumin, fennel, *kalonji,* and fenugreek — and bits of the new — onions, garlic, and tomatoes.

These potatoes, which have a thick sauce, generally are eaten with Indian breads along with other vegetables, yogurt relishes, chickpeas, and pickles.

SERVES 6

5 medium (about 1 3/4 pounds) waxy boiling potatoes, such as
*   Maine Eastern potatoes*
4 garlic cloves, peeled and coarsely chopped
A 2-inch piece of fresh ginger, peeled and coarsely chopped

6 tablespoons vegetable oil

A large pinch of ground asafetida

8 fenugreek seeds

1/2 teaspoon cumin seeds

1/2 teaspoon fennel seeds

1/4 teaspoon kalonji

1/4 teaspoon brown mustard seeds

1 bay leaf

1 medium onion, peeled and finely minced

2 ripe medium tomatoes, fresh or canned, finely chopped (if fresh, peeled and seeded first)

1/4 teaspoon cayenne pepper, or to taste

1 1/2 teaspoons salt

1 1/2 teaspoons lemon juice

1 teaspoon ground garam masala (page 20)

Boil the potatoes preferably 2 hours ahead, and leave to cool. Just before you begin cooking, peel the potatoes and break them by hand into 6 or 8 pieces each.

Put the garlic and ginger into a blender along with 3 tablespoons water. Blend until you have a paste.

Heat the oil in a wide pot over medium-high heat. When hot, add the asafetida and, a second later, the fenugreek, cumin, fennel, *kalonji*, mustard seeds, and bay leaf. As soon as the mustard seeds begin to pop — this takes just a few seconds — add the minced onion. Stir-fry until the onion just starts to brown. Add the garlic-ginger paste and fry for 4 to 5 minutes, stirring frequently. Add the tomatoes. Stir, and cook another 5 minutes. Now add the potatoes, 1 3/4 cups water, cayenne, salt, and lemon juice. Bring to a simmer, cover, lower heat, and cook gently for 15 to 20 minutes. The sauce should thicken. If it does not, uncover and cook another 5 minutes. Add the *garam masala* and stir gently to mix.

SPINACH WITH GINGER, FENNEL, AND BLACK CUMIN

Saag

The seasonings here are relatively simple. The flavor of fennel seeds and the more refined black cumin seeds are first intensified in hot oil. Then finely sliced onions and ginger shreds are allowed to brown in the same oil. Spinach is added and it slowly picks up all the flavor — those of the spices as well as those of browned onions and ginger. The heat comes form both a green chili and a touch of cayenne.

This spinach dish goes well with Chicken with Dried Fruit (page 82), Silken Chicken (page 80), Lamb in an Almond Sauce (page 92) and all the beef and pork dishes in this book. Rice and some chutney or relish would complete the meal. You could also serve the spinach as part of an all vegetarian meal along with Bazaar Potatoes (page 52), Chickpeas with Ginger and Cumin (page 62), Yogurt Raita with Roasted Cumin, (page 105) and Griddle Breads with Ajwain and Black Pepper (page 66).

SERVES 6

3 tablespoons vegetable oil

3 tablespoons unsalted butter

1/2 teaspoon fennel seeds

1 teaspoon black cumin seeds

2 medium onions, peeled, cut in half lengthwise, and then cut
  crosswise into thin fine half-rings

A 1-inch piece of fresh ginger, peeled and cut into very thin
  julienne strips

3 pounds fresh spinach, well washed

1 fresh long hot green chili or 1/3 jalapeño, cut into thin rings

1 teaspoon salt, or to taste

1/8 teaspoon cayenne pepper

Heat the oil and butter in a large pot over medium-high heat. When hot, put in the fennel and black cumin seeds. Stir once and add the onions and ginger. Stir-fry until the onions turn a rich, brown color. Then put in all the spinach, stuffing it into the pan if necessary. Cover and allow the spinach to wilt completely. Stir every now and then. When the spinach has wilted, turn the heat to medium. Add the chili, salt, and cayenne, stir, cover, and cook for 25 minutes.

Remove the lid and stir. Cook the spinach, uncovered, for another 5 minutes, or until there is hardly any liquid left in the bottom of the pan.

F e n n e l

TOMATOES COOKED WITH BENGALI SPICES

Bangali Timatar

This dish of stewed tomatoes is accented with a *tarka* (page 10) of the Bengali spice combination *panchphoran*, containing cumin, mustard, fennel, *kalonji*, and fenugreek seeds. If mustard oil is not available, a good extra-virgin olive oil will give an equally interesting flavor.

While ripe fresh tomatoes are best for this recipe, lightly drained canned tomatoes, with some juice included, may be substituted. (If too much canning juice is added, it will make the dish very watery.) If the canned tomatoes are large, cut them into 3/4-inch pieces. Plum tomatoes should be cut in half, while sliced tomatoes may be left the way they are.

This dish, which has a fair amount of liquid, is usually served in individual bowls. Serve it with rice and Delectable Pork in a Mustard Spice Mix (page 88) or a Whole Fish in Fresh Green Chutney (page 74).

SERVES 4 TO 6

2 pounds ripe tomatoes

3 tablespoons mustard oil or extra-virgin olive oil

6 fenugreek seeds

1/4 teaspoon cumin seeds

1/4 teaspoon fennel seeds

1/4 teaspoon brown mustard seeds

1/8 teaspoon kalonji

1 bay leaf

1/4 teaspoon cayenne pepper

1 teaspoon salt

1 1/2 teaspoons dark brown sugar

Bring 4 quarts of water to a boil in a large pot. Drop in the fresh tomatoes and remove them after 15 seconds. Peel the tomatoes and cut them in half crosswise. Gently squeeze out some of the seeds from the halves and then dice into 3/4-inch pieces.

Heat the oil in a heavy pot over medium-high heat. When hot, put in the fenugreek, cumin, fennel, mustard seeds, *kalonji,* and bay leaf. As soon as the mustard seeds pop — this takes just a few seconds — add the tomatoes and immediately cover the pot. (This keeps the aromatic fumes inside the pot.) Turn heat to medium. When tomatoes stop making noise from inside the pot, take off the lid and add the cayenne, salt, and brown sugar. Cover again, turn heat to low, and simmer 7 to 10 minutes, or until tomatoes are just cooked through.

F e n u g r e e k

ZUCCHINI IN A YOGURT DRESSING

Dahi May Zucchini

You may serve this dish cold, at room temperature, or warm. It is saladlike. The zucchini pieces are blanched — steam them if you prefer — and then smothered with yogurt that has been given a simple *tarka* of whole mustard seeds. A little roasted ground cumin and some cayenne are also added for extra flavor.

Serve this with Peshawari Kebabs (page 96), or Barbecued Leg of Lamb with a Spicy, Lemony Marinade (page 100), or with A Chicken, Legume, and Vegetable Stew (page 84). Rice or Griddle Breads (page 66) should be served on the side.　　SERVES 4

Salt

1 pound zucchini (2 medium), cut into 1/2-inch dice

3/4 cup plain yogurt

1/4 teaspoon cayenne pepper, or to taste

3/4 teaspoon ground roasted cumin seeds (page 18)

1/2 teaspoon brown or granulated sugar

1 tablespoon vegetable oil (mustard or extra-virgin olive oil)

1/2 teaspoon brown mustard seeds

Bring 2 1/2 quarts of water to a rolling boil. Add 1 tablespoon salt, stir, and put in the zucchini. Boil rapidly for 3 to 4 minutes, or until zucchini are just done. Drain and leave to cool.

Put the yogurt in a bowl and beat lightly with a fork until smooth. Add 1/4 teaspoon salt, the cayenne, roasted cumin, and sugar. Stir to mix.

Heat the oil in a very small pan or small skillet over fairly high heat. When very hot, add the mustard seeds. As soon as the mustard seeds begin to pop — this takes just a few seconds — pour the oil and seeds over the yogurt. Stir to mix. Gently fold the zucchini into the yogurt. Serve warm or cold.

LENTILS WITH CUMIN AND ASAFETIDA

Mili Dal

Indians tend to eat protein-rich legumes with many everyday meals. Often these are prepared simply with just a flavoring, or *tarka* (page 10), of cumin seeds, asafetida, and whole chilies popped in hot oil.

Serve this dish with plain rice and a simple meat or vegetable. Yogurt relishes and pickles make good accompaniments.

SERVES 4

1 cup red and yellow split lentils (masoor dal and mung dal) mixed in equal proportions, picked over, washed, and drained

1/2 teaspoon turmeric

3/4 teaspoon salt

3 tablespoons vegetable oil

A generous pinch of ground asafetida

1/2 teaspoon cumin seeds

2 – 3 dried hot red chilies

Put the lentils in a heavy pot with 2 1/2 cups water and the turmeric. Stir and bring to a simmer. (Do not let it boil over.) Cover, leaving the lid just very slightly ajar, turn heat to low, and simmer gently for 40 minutes, or until tender. Stir a few times during the cooking. Add the salt and mix. Leave covered over very low heat.

Heat the oil in a small frying pan over fairly high heat. When hot, add the asafetida, then, a second later, the cumin seeds. Let the cumin seeds sizzle for a few seconds. Add the chilies. As soon as they turn dark red — this takes just a few seconds — lift up the lid of the lentil pot and pour in the contents of the frying pan, oil as well as spices. Cover the pot immediately to trap the aromas.

LIMA BEANS WITH TOMATOES AND RAISINS

Hari Phali

The main spices in this dish are the thymelike *ajwain* and the sharper and more acrid cumin. They add just the right amount of seasoning to the fine balance of earthiness from the beans, gentle tartness from the tomatoes, and sweetness from the raisins.

To peel tomatoes, dip them into boiling water for 15 seconds. To seed them, cut them in half crosswise, and then gently squeeze out the seeds.

Serve with Chicken with Dried Fruit (page 82), or Lamb in a Tomato Sauce (page 94), or Beef Baked with Turnips and Black Pepper (page 98). Rice and a vegetable dish such as Stir-Fried Cauliflower with Ginger (page 44) would make an elegant meal.

SERVES 3 TO 4

1 10-ounce package frozen baby lima beans

3 tablespoons vegetable oil

A generous pinch of ground asafetida

1/2 teaspoon ajwain *seeds*

1/2 teaspoon cumin seeds

1/4 teaspoon turmeric

1/4 teaspoon cayenne pepper, or to taste

2 very ripe medium tomatoes, peeled, seeded, and finely chopped, or canned, drained tomatoes, chopped

1/2 – 3/4 teaspoon salt, or to taste

3 tablespoons golden raisins

2 teaspoons sugar

1 tablespoon lemon juice

Cook the lima beans according to package instructions but

without salt and for only 5 minutes. Drain.

Heat the oil in a medium pot over medium-high heat. When hot, add the asafetida and, a second later, the *ajwain* and cumin seeds. Stir once. Add the turmeric, cayenne, and tomatoes. Stir and cook for 3 minutes, or until tomatoes have softened. Add the drained lima beans, salt, raisins, sugar, and lemon juice. Stir to mix. Add 3/4 cup water and bring to a simmer. Cover tightly and simmer very gently for 30 minutes, or until lima beans are tender. Check the beans after every 10 minutes. If the liquid evaporates, add a tablespoon of hot water whenever needed. There should be just a little thick sauce by the time the lima beans are done.

C u m i n

CHICKPEAS WITH GINGER AND CUMIN

Dhabay Kay Chanay

Cooking in tea is the trick that all the vendors at truck stops use to give their chickpeas a traditional dark appearance. The tea — leftover tea may be used here — leaves no aftertaste. It just alters the color of the chickpeas.

For speed, I use canned chickpeas. As they are already cooked, they need just 10 minutes of gentle simmering to absorb the many flavorings, which are complex. The "wet trinity" — onion, garlic, and ginger — gives a basic sauce to the dish, the asafetida makes it digestible, and the roasted ground cumin and *garam masala* give a wonderful aroma.

This chickpea dish may be served with store-bought pita bread or Griddle Breads with *Awjain* and Black Pepper (page 66), a yogurt relish, and some pickles or salad. It could also be part of a more elaborate meal with meat or chicken, a green vegetable, and rice.

SERVES 4 TO 5

2 19-ounce cans chickpeas

4 tablespoons vegetable oil

A generous pinch of ground asafetida

1 teaspoon cumin seeds

2 medium onions, peeled and chopped

3 garlic cloves, peeled and finely chopped

5 tablespoons crushed canned tomatoes

2 teaspoons finely grated peeled fresh ginger

1 1/4 cups prepared tea (use a fairly plain tea) or water

1 – 2 fresh long hot green chilies cut into very thin rounds or 1/2 of a jalapeño, finely chopped

1 teaspoon salt

2 teaspoons ground roasted cumin seeds (page 18)

1 teaspoon ground garam masala *(page 20)*

3 – 4 tablespoons coarsely chopped green coriander (Chinese parsley, cilantro)

1 tablespoon lemon juice

Drain the chickpeas and rinse them gently with fresh water. Drain again.

Heat the oil in a wide pan over medium-high heat. When hot, add the asafetida and let it sizzle for a second. Add the cumin seeds and let them sizzle for about 15 seconds. Add the onions. Stir-fry until the onions turn quite brown at the edges. Add the garlic and stirring, let it turn golden. Add the tomatoes. Stir and cook until they turn dark and thick. Add the ginger and give a few good stirs. Add the chickpeas and all remaining ingredients. Bring to a simmer, turn heat to low, and simmer uncovered for about 10 minutes, stirring gently now and then. Taste for balance of flavors and make necessary adjustments.

A s a f e t i d a

YELLOW RICE WITH POTATO AND CUMIN

Peelay Chaaval

The yellow in this rice comes from turmeric (which happens to be a natural dye as well!) and the flavoring comes from the *tarka* of cumin and from the browned potato and onion.

This rice may be served with almost all main dishes in this book.

SERVES 4

1 1/2 cups basmati rice

3 tablespoons vegetable oil

1/2 teaspoon cumin seeds

1 tablespoon finely chopped onion

1 small boiling potato, boiled, cooled, peeled, and cut into 1/3-inch dice

1/2 teaspoon turmeric

3/4 teaspoon salt

Wash the rice in several changes of water. Drain. Soak the rice in water to cover generously and leave for 30 minutes. Drain thoroughly.

Heat the oil in a small, heavy pot over medium-high heat. When hot, add the cumin seeds and let them sizzle for 10 seconds. Now put in the onion. Stir and cook until it starts to brown. Add the potato. Stir it until it too is lightly browned. Put in the rice, turmeric, and salt. Turn heat to medium and stir the rice around gently for 2 minutes. Add 2 cups water and bring to a boil. Cover tightly, turn heat to very low, and cook for 25 minutes.

RICE AND PEAS WITH GARAM MASALA

Matar Aur Sooay Ka Pullao

The flavor in this rice dish comes from browned onions, fresh dill, and the aromatic *garam masala*. The combination of herbiness and spiciness is quite heady.

This elegant rice dish may be served with Chicken with Dried Fruit (page 82), Silken Chicken (page 80), or any pork or lamb dish in this book. I serve it all by itself as well, just as one might a risotto.

SERVES 5 TO 6

1 1/2 cups basmati rice

3 tablespoons vegetable oil

1 small onion, cut into thin half-rings

3/4 teaspoon salt

1 teaspoon ground garam masala (page 20)

4 tablespoons finely chopped fresh dill

2 cups chicken broth, fresh or canned

1 cup peas, fresh or frozen, cooked in boiling water for 2 minutes
   or until just done

Wash the rice in several changes of water and drain. Cover generously in water and soak for 30 minutes. Drain thoroughly.

Heat the oil in a small, heavy pot over medium-high heat. When hot, add the onion and stir until it is brown. Add the rice, salt, *garam masala*, and dill. Stir for a minute. Now put in the broth and bring to a boil. Cover very tightly, turn heat to very low, and cook 20 minutes.

Add the drained peas. Cover tightly again and cook another 5 to 7 minutes. Stir gently before serving.

GRIDDLE BREADS WITH AJWAIN AND BLACK PEPPER

Ajwain Ke Parathay

These layered breads, *parathas*, are cooked on a large griddle or cast-iron skillet and are flavored with the thymelike *ajwain* and black pepper. You can eat them with pickles and chutneys as a snack or, at mealtimes, serve them with vegetables, chickpeas, yogurt relishes, and meat dishes such as Chicken and Peas with Cinnamon and Bay Leaves (page 78) and Peshawari Kebabs (page 96).

MAKES 8 BREADS

1 3/4 cups unbleached white flour

1 3/4 cups whole wheat flour, sifted

1 teaspoon salt

2 teaspoons ajwain seeds

2 teaspoons coarsely ground black pepper

Extra white flour for dusting

1 cup melted butter or peanut oil

Put the two flours, salt, *ajwain*, and black pepper in a bowl. Slowly add about 1 1/4 cups water to make a very soft dough. Knead for 10 minutes. Cover and set aside for 2 to 4 hours. Knead again and divide into 8 balls. Cover 7 balls with plastic wrap or damp cloth as you work with the eighth.

Set a cast-iron skillet or griddle to heat on a fairly low flame.

Meanwhile, dust the work area with white flour. Place 1 ball of dough on it. Flatten it a bit and then roll it out until it measures 7 inches in diameter. Smear the surface with 1/2 teaspoon of the melted butter or oil. Dust a little flour over the top. Roll the round towards you tightly so you end up with a "snake." Coil the snake around itself tightly, spiraling upwards in a cone shape. Push down the spiral to form a patty. Dust the patty lightly with flour and roll

YELLOW RICE WITH POTATO AND CUMIN

Peelay Chaaval

The yellow in this rice comes from turmeric (which happens to be a natural dye as well!) and the flavoring comes from the *tarka* of cumin and from the browned potato and onion.

This rice may be served with almost all main dishes in this book.

SERVES 4

1 1/2 cups basmati rice

3 tablespoons vegetable oil

1/2 teaspoon cumin seeds

1 tablespoon finely chopped onion

1 small boiling potato, boiled, cooled, peeled, and cut into 1/3-inch dice

1/2 teaspoon turmeric

3/4 teaspoon salt

Wash the rice in several changes of water. Drain. Soak the rice in water to cover generously and leave for 30 minutes. Drain thoroughly.

Heat the oil in a small, heavy pot over medium-high heat. When hot, add the cumin seeds and let them sizzle for 10 seconds. Now put in the onion. Stir and cook until it starts to brown. Add the potato. Stir it until it too is lightly browned. Put in the rice, turmeric, and salt. Turn heat to medium and stir the rice around gently for 2 minutes. Add 2 cups water and bring to a boil. Cover tightly, turn heat to very low, and cook for 25 minutes.

RICE A[...] GA[...]

Matar [...]

The flavor in this rice dish c[...] and the aromatic *garam masa[...]* spiciness is quite heady.

This elegant rice dish may b[...] Fruit (page 82), Silken Chicken [...] dish in this book. I serve it all by i[...] risotto.

1 1/2 cups basmati rice

3 tablespoons vegetable oil

1 small onion, cut into thin half-rings

3/4 teaspoon salt

1 teaspoon ground garam masala (page 20[...]

4 tablespoons finely chopped fresh dill

2 cups chicken broth, fresh or canned

1 cup peas, fresh or frozen, cooked in boiling w[...] or until just done

Wash the rice in several changes of water and [...] generously in water and soak for 30 minutes. Drain th[...]

Heat the oil in a small, heavy pot over medium-[...] When hot, add the onion and stir until it is brown. Add[...] salt, *garam masala*, and dill. Stir for a minute. Now pu[...] broth and bring to a boil. Cover very tightly, turn heat to ve[...] and cook 20 minutes.

Add the drained peas. Cover tightly again and cook anoth[...] to 7 minutes. Stir gently before serving.

GRIDD[...]

These layer[...] cast-iron sk[...] black pepp[...] snack or, [...] yogurt re[...] Cinnamo[...] 96).

1 3[...]
1 3[...]
1 [...]
2 [...]

out into a 7 1/2-inch round.

When the skillet is well heated, slap the bread onto it. Let it sit for 30 seconds. Lift it up slightly with a spatula and drizzle 1 teaspoon butter or oil under it. Make a wad from a clean dish cloth or paper towel and press down on different sections of the bread, turning it slightly in the same direction each time you do this. Cook this way for 2 to 3 minutes, or until the bottom of the bread has reddish-brown spots. Drizzle 1 teaspoon butter or oil on top of the bread and flip it over. Press down again with the wad as you turn the bread. Cook this side for 3 minutes, or until it too has reddish-brown spots. When done, wrap in foil.

Make all breads this way. Stacked breads, wrapped in foil, may be heated by placing stack in a 350° F. oven for 15 minutes. An individual bread may be heated, uncovered, in a microwave for 1 minute.

B l a c k   P e p p e r

PLAIN BASMATI RICE

Saaday Chaaval

This is one of the simplest ways of preparing basmati rice. There are no seasonings in it except for a few cardamom pods to provide aroma. These pods are never eaten. This rice may be served with all Indian meals.

SERVES 4

1 1/2 cups basmati rice
3 cardamom pods

Put the rice in a bowl and wash in several changes of water. Drain. Cover well with water and leave to soak for 30 minutes. Drain thoroughly.

Put the rice, 2 cups water, and the cardamom pods in a small, heavy pot and bring to a boil. Cover tightly, reduce heat to very low, and cook for 25 minutes without removing the lid. Fluff and serve.

Cardamom

SEAFOOD, FISH, AND CHICKEN

SHRIMP IN MUSTARD SEED AND GREEN CHILI SAUCE

Chingri Bhapey

Very few people in the West associate the technique of gentle steaming with Indian cuisine. And yet in many regions of India, such as the East and the South, steaming is common and steaming utensils are standard equipment in every kitchen.

This simple, yet stunning dish is a Bengali classic. Fish — in Bengal it can be pieces of hilsa, a kind of freshwater mackerel, or shrimp — are smothered with a paste of crushed mustard seeds and mustard oil and left to steam briefly just until the fish turns opaque. The results are spectacular. The fish turns silken and the sauce created by the steam and the sweating fish is magically sweet and pungent. The dish is always eaten with plain rice. Tangy Green Beans with *Ajwain* and Ginger (page 38) may be served on the side.

Mustard oil is good to know about. Pungent when raw, it turns comfortingly sweet when heated. It is sold by Indian grocers. If you can't find it, use a good virgin olive oil instead. The taste is different but the intensity is the same. Good-quality fish is essential here. You may use pieces of fresh haddock instead of the shrimp if you so desire.

Use one of two methods for steaming: (1) Put the bowl of shrimp into a large pot. Pour boiling water into the pot so it comes one-third of the way up the sides of the bowl. Cover the pot and steam over medium heat. (2) Put water in the bottom third of a large wok. Bring to a boil. Put a bamboo steaming tray or perforated metal steaming tray on top of the water. Place the bowl of shrimp on the tray, cover wok, and steam over high heat.

SERVES 4

1 pound medium shrimp
1 1/2 teaspoons brown mustard seeds
1 tablespoon finely chopped onion

1 fresh long hot green chili or 1/3 jalapeño, finely chopped
1/4 teaspoon turmeric
1/4 teaspoon salt
1/4 teaspoon cayenne pepper
3 tablespoons mustard oil or virgin olive oil

Peel and devein the shrimp. Wash and drain.

Grind the mustard seeds coarsely in a clean coffee grinder or other spice grinder. Put into a medium stainless steel, ceramic, or heatproof glass bowl. Add 1 tablespoon water and mix. Mix in the onion, chili, turmeric, salt, cayenne, and oil. Now mix in the shrimp. Cover with a piece of foil and set aside for 10 minutes as you get your steaming equipment ready. Steam, covered, for 10 to 15 minutes, or until the shrimp just turn opaque all the way through. Stir the shrimp once after about 6 minutes, remembering to cover the bowl and the steaming utensil afterwards.

M u s t a r d

SHRIMP IN A CREAMY AROMATIC SAUCE

Bhagari Jhinga

Mustard seeds are dropped into very hot oil for a few seconds to allow them to pop and turn nutty, some garlic is stirred in, and then peeled shrimp are added and tossed with the garlic and mustard until they are almost done. With the addition of some salt, black pepper, and cayenne, this could be a simple dish in itself. Instead comes the silken sauce — a tomato and cream base with the earthy addition of ground roasted cumin, pungent fresh ginger, lemon juice, and the aromatic *garam masala*.

The sauce can be made ahead of time and refrigerated. The shrimp can be peeled, deveined, washed, and patted dry and left covered in the refrigerator. The actual cooking takes just a few minutes.

This dish is best served with rice — any rice dish in this book will do. A salad or Tangy Green Beans with *Ajwain* and Ginger (page 38) would also go well with it.

SERVES 4 TO 5

For the Sauce

1 cup canned tomato sauce

3/4 teaspoon salt

1 teaspoon ground garam masala *(page 20)*

1/2 teaspoon ground roasted cumin seeds *(page 18)*

1/8 – 1/4 teaspoon cayenne pepper, or to taste

1 teaspoon peeled and very finely grated fresh ginger

3 tablespoons finely chopped green coriander (Chinese parsley, cilantro)

1 fresh long hot green chili or 1/2 jalapeño, finely chopped

1 tablespoon lemon juice

1 cup heavy cream

For the Shrimp

3 tablespoons vegetable oil

1 teaspoon brown mustard seeds

3 garlic cloves, peeled and finely chopped

1 1/4 pounds medium shrimp, peeled and deveined, washed, and
patted dry

Put the tomato sauce in a bowl. Add the salt, *garam masala,* ground cumin, cayenne, ginger, coriander, chili, lemon juice, and cream. Mix well, cover, and set aside, refrigerating if necessary.

Just before you sit down to eat, heat the oil in a wok or a frying pan over fairly high heat. When hot, add the mustard seeds. As soon as the mustard seeds begin to pop — this takes just a few seconds — add the garlic. Stir briefly, until the garlic turns medium-brown, then add the shrimp. Stir until the shrimp turn opaque most of the way through, then add the sauce. Turn heat to medium and heat the sauce through just until it begins to simmer. By then the shrimp should be completely opaque and cooked through. Turn off the heat. Serve.

C o r i a n d e r

WHOLE FISH IN FRESH GREEN CHUTNEY

Hare Masale Ki Macchi

Indian chutneys come in many guises and are at the table, in some form or other, at almost every meal. They may be used as a relish, as a dressing, or in the actual cooking, as is done here. This vitamin-rich fresh chutney, rather like Italian pesto, is made up of fresh herbs and seasonings. The main herb here is lots of green coriander (Chinese parsley, cilantro), which is ground up with garlic, ginger, and green chilies and then flavored with a *tarka* (page 10) of cumin seeds, mustard seeds, and turmeric. This paste is then used to smother a whole fish and bake it.

You could serve this with Spicy, Sour Potatoes with Cumin and *Amchoor* (page 50) or a rice dish as well as Carrots with Raisins, *Ajwain*, and Mint (page 41).

SERVES 2

1 cup chopped green coriander (Chinese parsley, cilantro)

A piece of fresh ginger, 1 inch long and 1 inch wide, peeled and coarsely chopped

3 garlic cloves, peeled and coarsely chopped

1-2 fresh, long, hot green chilies or 1/3 – 3/4 jalapeño, coarsely chopped

2 tablespoons lemon juice

2 tablespoons olive or other vegetable oil

1/2 teaspoon cumin seeds

1/2 teaspoon brown mustard seeds

1/2 teaspoon turmeric

1/2 teaspoon salt

1 whole fish, 1 1/2 – 2 pounds, with head and tail on but otherwise cleaned (sea bass, striped bass, talapia, trout, small salmon, red snapper, pompano)

Preheat the oven to 400° F.

Place the coriander, ginger, garlic, and chili in a blender along with the lemon juice and 1 to 2 tablespoons of water. Blend at a high speed until you have a smooth paste.

Heat the oil in a small pot over medium-high heat, and add the cumin and mustard seeds. Within a few seconds, they will begin to expand and pop. Add the turmeric and stir once. Quickly pour the contents of the pot — oil and spices — over the coriander paste. Add the salt and mix.

Line a large baking dish with a sheet of heavy-duty aluminum foil large enough to fold over the fish. Cut 4 deep, somewhat diagonal slits on each side of the fish and place it on the foil. Smother the fish with the green paste, inside and out. Fold the foil over so the fish is completely enclosed in it. Place in the oven and bake 30 minutes.

C h i l i e s

SALMON POACHED WITH SPINACH AND BENGALI FIVE-SPICE MIXTURE

Panchphoran Vali Macchi

In Bengal, the five whole spices frequently used as a *tarka* (page 10) for seasoning fish and vegetables are fennel, fenugreek, *kalonji*, cumin, and mustard seeds. These seeds may be bought pre-mixed and are collectively known as *panchphoran*. Of course, you can just as easily mix your own. They provide the main flavor here, along with ginger and garlic.

The fish I have chosen to use is salmon, as it holds its shape and has a fine flavor. However, you could use thick pieces of filleted haddock, halibut, or cod as well.

Serve with any rice dish and perhaps Stir-Fried Cauliflower with Ginger (page 44).

SERVES 5 TO 6

1 1/2 pounds salmon fillet (preferably the thick center section), skin removed

Salt

Freshly ground black pepper

4 tablespoons vegetable oil

1/4 teaspoon cumin seeds

1/4 teaspoon brown mustard seeds

1/4 teaspoon fennel seeds

1/8 teaspoon fenugreek seeds

1/8 teaspoon kalonji

A large onion, peeled and cut in half lengthwise and then cross wise into thin half-rings

A 1 1/2-inch cube of fresh ginger, peeled and cut into very thin slices and then into very fine slivers

1 pound trimmed fresh spinach, finely shredded

8 canned plum tomatoes, chopped, or fresh tomatoes, peeled and
seeded
1/2 cup heavy cream
1/4 teaspoon cayenne pepper, or to taste

Cut the salmon fillet crosswise into 5 or 6 portions (as many as there are people). Pull out bones, if any, with a pair of tweezers. Sprinkle salt and pepper on both sides of the fish pieces and set aside for 20 minutes or longer.

Heat the oil in a very large frying pan or a very wide sauté pan over medium-high heat. When very hot, add the cumin, mustard seeds, fennel, fenugreek, and *kalonji*. Stir once or twice and quickly add the onion and ginger. Stir until the onion just starts to brown, then add the spinach. Sauté for about 5 minutes, then add the tomatoes. Continue to sauté for another 4 to 5 minutes. Add the cream and 2 cups water, cayenne, 1 teaspoon salt, and some black pepper. Stir to mix and bring to a simmer. Simmer, uncovered, over low heat for 5 minutes. (This much of the recipe can be done ahead of time.)

Just before you sit down to eat, bring the sauce to a simmer again. Lay the fish pieces in a single layer over the sauce. Spoon some of the thinner, more watery parts of the sauce over the fish. Cover. Simmer for 5 to 10 minutes, or until the fish has just cooked through.

F e n n e l

CHICKEN AND PEAS WITH CINNAMON AND BAY LEAVES

Murghi Ka Keema

Ground chicken — or turkey, for that matter — cooks in minutes. If a guest unexpectedly shows up, this may be the perfect dish to serve. I have used peas here, but infinite variations are possible — cooked lima beans, cut-up and cooked green beans, even corn kernels.

The spices used are some whole *garam masalas*, the wet trinity of onion, garlic, and ginger, as well as some of the *rai masala* with mustard and fenugreek seeds.

This simple dish may be served with rice and Lentils with Cumin and Asafetida (page 59).

SERVES 3 TO 4

3 tablespoons vegetable oil

A 1-inch piece of cinnamon

4 cardamom pods

2 bay leaves

1 medium onion, peeled and chopped

3 garlic cloves, peeled and finely chopped

2 teaspoons peeled and finely grated ginger

1 1/4 pounds ground chicken or turkey

1 1/4 cups lightly cooked peas, fresh or frozen

1/4 teaspoon turmeric

1 teaspoon rai masala (page 23)

1/4 teaspoon cayenne pepper

1/2 – 3/4 teaspoon salt

2 tablespoons lemon juice

Freshly ground black pepper

Heat the oil in a wide pan over medium-high heat. When hot, add the cinnamon, cardamom, and bay leaves. Stir for a few seconds. Add the onion. Stir-fry until the onion turns brown at the edges. Add the garlic and stir for a few seconds. Add the ginger and stir another few seconds. Now add the chicken or turkey. Stir-fry until all the lumps are broken up. Now add all the remaining ingredients, stir to mix, and cook another 2 to 3 minutes, stirring as you do so. Remove the large pieces of spice before serving.

Cinnamon

SILKEN CHICKEN

Reshmi Murgh

Broiled and roasted meats, especially those that cook as fast as this chicken does, often require a period of marination to allow spices and seasonings to penetrate the flesh. This way, the varied aromas of the *garam masala* spices and the tastes of the ginger, garlic, and roasted cumin get right into the meat, permeating it.

This dish, however simple its preparation (it cooks in just 15 minutes), has complex flavors. The spices and seasonings in the marinade mingle with the cream and have a subtle effect. The spices that are sprinkled over the top of the chicken — including a repeat of the aromatic *garam masala* and the nutty ground roasted cumin as well as the sour *amchoor* — hit the mouth right away and have a more immediate and intense impact.

These chicken breasts may be served Indian-style with rice and vegetables or Western-style with boiled potatoes and either steamed vegetables or a salad.

SERVES 2 TO 4

For Marinating the Chicken

4 boneless and skinless chicken breast halves (about 1 1/4 pounds)

1/2 teaspoon salt

2 tablespoons lemon juice

4 tablespoons heavy cream

1/2 teaspoon ground garam masala (page 20)

1/4 teaspoon cayenne pepper

1 garlic clove, peeled and mashed

1/2 teaspoon peeled and finely grated fresh ginger

1/4 teaspoon ground roasted cumin seeds (page 18)

Generous squeezes of lemon juice

A generous pinch of salt

Freshly ground black pepper

A generous pinch of ground garam masala *(page 20)*

A generous pinch of ground roasted cumin seeds (page 18)

Pinch of cayenne pepper

1/2 teaspoon amchoor *powder, well crumbled*

Cut 3 diagonal slits across the top of each piece of chicken, being careful not to go through the meat and also careful not to cut to the edge. Prick the chicken pieces with the sharp point of a small knife. Lay the chicken in a large, fairly deep plate in a single layer and rub both sides with the salt and lemon juice. Leave for 10 to 15 minutes.

Meanwhile, combine the cream, *garam masala*, cayenne, garlic, ginger, and cumin in a bowl. Stir and pour over the chicken. Rub the marinade into the meat and leave for 10 minutes or longer — up to 12 hours, covering and refrigerating if necessary.

Preheat the oven to its highest temperature and arrange a shelf in the top third of the oven.

Lay the chicken pieces in a single layer on a shallow baking tray with foil. Most of the marinade will cling to them. On top of each piece, sprinkle the lemon juice, salt, black pepper, *garam masala*, ground roasted cumin, cayenne, and *amchoor.*

When the oven is hot, put the chicken on the high shelf and bake 15 minutes, or until just white all the way through. Serve immediately.

CHICKEN WITH DRIED FRUIT

Shahi Murgh

This is a mild and elegant dish that may be served to the family or at a grand party. The main flavors come from the yogurt — which disappears but leaves traces of its creamy tartness; the golden raisins, which give a wonderful sweetness; and the almonds, which provide a toasted nuttiness. Browning the chicken with the whole *garam masala* makes it extra flavorful. The green coriander provides a note of cleansing freshness. Rice is the ideal accompaniment. A vegetable such as green beans, cabbage, or cauliflower should be served on the side.

SERVES 4

1 cup plain yogurt

1 teaspoon salt

Freshly ground black pepper

1 teaspoon ground cumin

1 teaspoon ground coriander

1/4 teaspoon cayenne pepper, or to taste

4 tablespoons minced green coriander (Chinese parsley, cilantro)

3 1/2 pounds chicken pieces (preferably thighs but all parts will do)

4 tablespoons vegetable oil

8 cardamom pods

6 whole cloves

A 2-inch cinnamon stick

3 bay leaves

2 1/2 tablespoons blanched slivered almonds

2 1/2 tablespoons golden raisins

Put the yogurt in a bowl and beat it lightly until smooth and creamy. Add 1/2 teaspoon of the salt, some black pepper, the cumin, coriander, cayenne, and green coriander. Mix and set aside.

Salt and pepper the chicken pieces on both sides using the remaining 1/2 teaspoon salt.

Heat the oil in a wide, preferably nonstick pan over medium-high heat. When hot, add the cardamom, cloves, cinnamon, and bay leaves. Stir once and add as many chicken pieces as the pan will hold easily in a single layer. Brown the chicken on both sides and set aside in a large bowl. Brown all the chicken this way and remove to the bowl.

Into the same hot oil, add the almonds and raisins. Stir quickly. The almonds should turn golden and the raisins should plump up — this should happen very fast. Put the chicken and its accumulated juices back into the pan. Add the seasoned yogurt. Stir to mix and bring to a simmer. Cover, turn heat to low, and simmer gently for 20 minutes, stirring once or twice. Remove cover, turn the heat up a bit, and reduce the sauce until it is thick and just clings to the chicken pieces, turning the chicken pieces over gently as you do so. Remove large whole spices before serving.

C l o v e s

A CHICKEN, LEGUME, AND VEGETABLE STEW

Ek Handi Ka Murgh Aur Dal

Almost everything you need for a meal, except the rice or bread, is cooked in one pot — poultry, lentils, green vegetable, even tomatoes. If you leave out the chilies and cayenne pepper, this is a perfect dish for children as well.

This dish has two families of spices in it: aromatic whole *garam masalas*, associated with North Indian meat and rice dishes, and asafetida and whole cumin, which are associated with legumes. Asafetida is the all-important digestive used in most dried bean dishes. The final *tarka* (page 10) that is thrown over the cooked food like a benediction is somewhat elaborate this time. Not only are cumin and asafetida dropped into the hot oil, but sliced onions, garlic, ground cumin, and coriander and cherry tomatoes as well. This *tarka* perks up the stew and makes it sing. As each of these seasonings has a different tolerance to the heat of the oil, they are added in a special sequence, with the whole spices going before the ground, powdery ones.

SERVES 4 TO 6

6 tablespoons vegetable oil

3 bay leaves

5 whole cloves

6 cardamom pods

A 2-inch stick of cinnamon

3 hot dried red chilies

2 pounds chicken parts with bone, skinned and cut into smaller serving pieces (whole legs into 2 and a pair of breasts into 4 – 6 pieces — the butcher could do this for you)

1 1/2 cups red and yellow split lentils (masoor and moong dal), in equal proportions picked over, washed, and drained

1/2 teaspoon turmeric

Salt

Freshly ground black pepper

1 1/2 teaspoons rai masala *(page 23)*

1 1/2 tablespoons lemon juice

6 ounces green beans, trimmed and cut into 1-inch lengths

A generous pinch of asafetida (optional)

1 1/2 teaspoons cumin seeds

1 medium onion, peeled and cut into thin half-rings

2 garlic cloves, peeled and finely chopped

1 teaspoon ground cumin

1 teaspoon ground coriander

1/8 – 1/4 teaspoon cayenne pepper (optional)

12 cherry tomatoes, cut into halves crosswise

Put 3 tablespoons of the oil in a wide nonstick pot and heat over high heat. When hot, add the bay leaves, cloves, cardamom pods, cinnamon stick, and chilies. Stir once or twice, until the bay leaf starts to darken. Quickly add the chicken pieces in a single layer and brown on both sides. Remove the chicken from the oil and spices and spread it out on a plate.

Take the pot briefly off the fire and add the lentils, turmeric, and 5 cups water. Put it back over high heat and bring to a simmer. Cover partly and cook gently for 30 minutes.

Meanwhile, sprinkle on both sides of the chicken pieces 1/2 teaspoon salt, lots of black pepper, 1/2 teaspoon of the *rai masala*, and the lemon juice. Rub it in and set aside. When lentils have cooked for 20 minutes, put in the chicken and all accumulated juices, the green beans, and 1 1/4 teaspoons salt. Stir and bring to a simmer. Cover, turn heat to low, and cook gently for another 25 minutes, stirring now and then.

Heat the remaining 3 tablespoons oil in a medium frying pan over high heat. When hot, add the asafetida and, a second later, the cumin seeds. Ten seconds later, add the onion. Stir-fry until the onion turns brown at the edges. Add the garlic. Stir-fry until the onion has turned fairly brown. Add the ground cumin, coriander, remaining 1 teaspoon *rai masala,* and the cayenne if you want the dish to be hot. Stir once. Now add the tomatoes, stir for 30 seconds, and pour this entire mixture into the pot with the chicken and lentils. Stir to mix.

B a y   L e a v e s

PORK, LAMB, AND BEEF

DELECTABLE PORK IN A MUSTARD SPICE MIX

Boti Gosht

This exquisite dish has no sauce. The meat cubes are almost like kebabs, except that they are not grilled but cooked in a pot. Many flavorings cling to them — fresh ginger and garlic, as well a wonderful mixture of ground cumin, coriander, mustard, cayenne, and fenugreek. It is the last three, and the green chilies, that give the kebabs an earthy pungency. After the cooking is completed, lots of black pepper and lemon juice are sprinkled over the top providing an outer layer of flavor.

I like to make this dish with boned pork shoulder cut into cubes. Boned lamb shoulder would work equally well.

You could serve this as part of an Indian meal with rice and a vegetable such as Eggplant Baked in a Sweet-and-Sour Tamarind Sauce (page 46), Peas with Whole Cumin and Mustard Seeds (page 48), or Western-style, with boiled or mashed potatoes, broiled tomatoes, and a green salad.

SERVES 3 TO 4

3 tablespoons vegetable oil

A 1 1/2-inch piece of fresh ginger, peeled and very finely minced

4 garlic cloves, peeled and very finely minced

1 pound boneless pork meat from the shoulder, cut into 1-inch cubes

2 teaspoons rai masala *(page 23)*

1 teaspoon ground cumin

1/4 teaspoon turmeric

1/4 teaspoon cayenne pepper

1 fresh long hot green chili (or 1/2 jalapeño), thinly sliced

1/2 teaspoon salt, or to taste

Lots of freshly ground black pepper
1 1/2 – 2 teaspoons lemon juice

Heat the oil in a wide pot or large skillet over medium-high heat. When hot, add the ginger and garlic. Stir. When the garlic starts to brown, add the meat. Stir once or twice and turn the heat to medium low. Now add the *rai masala,* cumin, turmeric, cayenne, chili, and salt. Stir to mix. Add 1 cup water and bring to a boil. Cover tightly, turn heat to low, and simmer gently for 50 to 60 minutes, or until the pork is almost done. Remove cover. Cook, uncovered, over high heat until all the liquid is gone and the meat has browned a bit, stirring as you do so. Add lots of freshly ground pepper and the lemon juice. Stir to mix.

Turmeric

PORK IN A TAMARIND SAUCE

Khatta Gosht

You already know from any Mediterranean cooking you have done that if you drop slivers of garlic into hot oil and brown them lightly, the garlic taste becomes intensified and that taste then permeates the oil. Anything cooked in that oil has an intense garlic flavor and aroma. The same thing happens with whole spices such as black peppercorns, cinnamon sticks, cloves, and dried chilies. It is worth noting that because the chilies are whole, only the earthy flavor of the browned skin is picked up.

Here, I have used this technique for cooking these sweet-and-sour pork chops. The combination of the whole *garam masala* spices with sour tamarind paste and pork is quite heavenly. It is best to use thin-cut loin pork chops for this recipe. Most supermarkets sell them.

This dish may be served with Rice and Peas with *Garam Masala* (page 65) and Stir-Fried Cauliflower with Ginger (page 44). You may also serve it Western-style, with plain rice and a salad.

SERVES 4

2-3 tablespoons vegetable oil

8 thin-cut loin pork chops

1 teaspoon black peppercorns

8 whole cloves

2 cinnamon sticks, each 2 1/2 inches long

10 cardamom pods

2 garlic cloves, peeled

1 – 2 dried hot red chilies

1 – 1 1/2 teaspoons salt

2 tablespoons tamarind paste (page 108)

2 teaspoons sugar

Heat the oil in a 10- or 12-inch heavy-bottomed pot over medium-high heat. When oil is very hot, put in 4 pork chops at a time and brown them on both sides. This should take 3 to 4 minutes on each side. Once the pork chops have browned, remove them to a side dish. Lower the heat to medium.

In the same oil, add first the peppercorns, then the cloves, cinnamon, cardamom pods, garlic, and chilies. Stir-fry for about a minute or less, until chilies darken and the garlic is a bit browned.

Return the pork chops to the skillet and add 1 cup water, 1 teaspoon salt, tamarind paste, and sugar. Bring to a boil, cover, lower heat, and cook very gently for 50 minutes. Turn the chops over a few times as they cook.

Uncover and taste for salt, adding more if needed. Turn heat to high and boil off most of the liquid, leaving just the oil behind. Turn the pork chops gently as you do this.

Lift the chops from the pot with a slotted spoon when serving, leaving all the oil and spices behind.

T a m a r i n d

LAMB IN AN ALMOND SAUCE

Gosht Badami

This is a classic North Indian Muslim dish in which the sauce is prepared in several stages. Most of the spices, such as the cumin, coriander, cloves, nutmeg, and cardamom, as well as the almonds and coconut, are roasted before being ground; this is what gives the sauce its dark color and nutty taste. They are combined with ground garlic, ginger, and fried onions and then sautéed with the addition of a small amount of yogurt to thicken the sauce and give it a slight tartness.

Even though shoulder of lamb is used here, you could use neck or shank. Stewing beef may also be substituted, though you would need to cook it for 1 1/2 hours.

This classic dish may be served with rice, or store-bought pita bread. A vegetable such as Spinach with Ginger, Fennel, and Black Cumin (page 54) or Stir-Fried Cauliflower with Ginger (page 44) would go well with it, as will Yogurt Raita with Tomato and Cucumber (page 104). If serving rice, Lentils with Cumin and Asafetida (page 59) might be added.

SERVES 4 TO 6

8 whole cloves

1 – 2 dried hot red chilies

1/2 teaspoon black peppercorns

8 cardamom pods

1/3 nutmeg

A 1/2-inch piece of mace

2 teaspoons cumin seeds

1 1/2 tablespoons coriander seeds

1 tablespoon unsweetened, dried, shredded coconut

3 tablespoons coarsely chopped blanched almonds

6 garlic cloves, peeled and coarsely chopped

A 1-inch cube of fresh ginger, peeled and coarsely chopped

1/2 teaspoon turmeric

6 tablespoons vegetable oil

2 pounds boneless meat from shoulder of lamb, cut into 1-inch cubes

2 medium onions, peeled and finely minced

3 tablespoons plain yogurt

1/2 cup canned tomato sauce

1 1/2 teaspoons salt

Combine the cloves, chilies, peppercorns, cardamom, nutmeg, mace, cumin, coriander, coconut, and almonds in a cast-iron skillet over medium heat. Stir until all the spices are lightly toasted, about 5 minutes. Let spices cool a bit, then grind finely in a clean coffee grinder or other spice grinder. You may need to do this in more than one batch.

Put the garlic, ginger, turmeric, and 1/2 cup water into the blender and blend until smooth.

Heat the oil in a wide, heavy pot over fairly high heat. When hot, put in 7 or 8 pieces of meat at a time to brown. When each batch is brown on all sides, remove with a slotted spoon and place in a bowl. Continue to brown all the meat this way and set aside.

Put the onions into the same pot and cook over high heat, stirring and scraping up the juices for about 5 minutes, or until they turn dark in spots. Then lower the heat to medium and add the paste from blender as well as the ground spices. Stir-fry for 5 minutes, gradually adding the yogurt as you do so, 1 tablespoon at a time.

Add the tomato sauce and 1/2 cup water. Bring to a boil. Cover, lower heat, and simmer gently for 15 minutes.

Add the meat and all accumulated juices to the sauce. Add the salt and stir. Bring to a boil, cover, lower heat, and simmer gently for 1 hour. Stir a few times as it cooks.

LAMB IN A TOMATO SAUCE

Elaichi Gosht

Indian foods can be spicy without being hot. In this Sindhi dish from Western India, the main flavoring is cardamom. Two whole tablespoons are used. The green cardamom pods are ground whole, skin and all. This may be done in a clean coffee-grinder or other spice grinder or even in a good-quality blender. The seeds provide pungency and an intense, flowery aroma while the skin adds a gentler aroma and a lot of body.

The mild, aromatic dish — it has no red chilies but a good amount of black pepper — is very much like a stew, gentle and soothing. In fact, for this very reason, it is often served to people who are feeling slightly "under the weather." It should have quite a bit of sauce. Sindhis like to sop up the sauce with plenty of Western-style bread so serving thick slices from a good, crusty Italian or French loaf on the side would be downright "authentic". You may serve a simple green salad on the side or else a selection of Indian vegetables such as Stir-Fried Cauliflower with Ginger (page 44) and Spinach with Ginger, Fennel and Black Cumin (page 54).

SERVES 6

2 tablespoons cardamom pods

3 tablespoons vegetable oil

2 pounds boneless lamb from the shoulder, cut into 1-inch cubes

2 large, ripe tomatoes, chopped

4 tablespoons finely chopped onion (preferably red onion or shallot)

1 1/2 teaspoons rai masala (page 23)

1 tablespoon tomato paste

1 1/2 teaspoons salt, or to taste

Freshly ground black pepper

Using a clean coffee grinder or other spice grinder, grind the whole cardamom pods, skin and all, into a fine powder.

Heat the oil in a wide, heavy pot over medium-high heat. When hot, add the cardamom powder. Stir once and add the meat. Stir over high heat for 2 minutes. Add the tomatoes and onion. Stir another 3 minutes. Now add the *rai masala*, tomato paste, salt, and 2 1/2 cups water. Bring to a boil. Cover tightly, lower heat, and simmer gently for 1 hour and 10 minutes, or until lamb is tender. Grind in a very generous amount of black pepper and cook, stirring gently, for a minute. Check for salt.

C a r d a m o m

PESHAWARI KEBABS

Chappal Kabab

These kebabs — actually spicy hamburgers — are a snack food and meant to be fairly hot. This heat comes from fresh green chilies. I have used just 2 cayenne-type chilies, but you could use one whole chili per kebab if you are up to it. For the same amount of heat, use about half a jalapeño pepper. To counter the heat is the lovely freshness of green coriander, which is used fairly generously.

The other spices include cumin and coriander seeds, which add both taste and crunch. Coriander seeds are rarely used whole except in pickles and snacks, where they sit in the food like little round pellets of flavor, waiting to explode in the mouth.

These kebabs may be eaten with rice and vegetables, but they are best cut in half and rolled up in a flat bread, such as store-bought pita or Griddle Breads with *Ajwain* and Black Pepper (page 66), along with a little salad and some Red Pepper Chutney with Mint and Almonds (page 107). You could also eat them like a hamburger, in a hamburger bun. Again, a little salad and fresh chutney should be sandwiched in as well.

Small versions of these kebabs may be served with drinks.

MAKES 10 THIN, HAMBURGER KEBABS,
SERVING 4 TO 5

1 1/2 pounds ground beef or lamb, put through the grinder 3
    times until fine
6 – 7 tablespoons coarsely chopped green coriander (Chinese
    parsley, cilantro)
2 or more fresh long hot green chilies cut into thin rounds and
    then chopped or 1 jalapeño, finely chopped
1 1/2 teaspoons cumin seeds

1 1/2 teaspoons coriander seeds

1 teaspoon freshly ground black pepper

1 1/4 teaspoons salt

1/2 lightly beaten egg

3 – 4 tablespoons vegetable oil

Put the meat into a bowl. Add all the other ingredients except the oil and mix well. Form ten 2-inch balls, then flatten the balls to make ten 3 1/2-inch hamburgerlike discs.

Just before eating, heat 2 tablespoons oil in a large nonstick frying pan and heat over medium-high heat. When hot, put in as many kebabs as the pan will hold in a single layer. Turning them over every 30 seconds or so, cook the kebabs for about 2 1/2 minutes, or until they have browned on both sides. Remove to a warm plate. Use the remaining oil to cook a second batch the same way.

C o r i a n d e r

BEEF BAKED WITH TURNIPS AND BLACK PEPPER

Shaljum Vala Dum Gosht

Here, I use a traditional Moghul method of cooking that dates back to the sixteenth century. Meat is browned and then put into a heavy pot with yogurt, turnips, and relatively mild seasonings such as browned onions and garlic, black pepper, and ground coriander. In the old days, the pot was covered with a flat lid, sealed shut with dough, and then placed over a gentle fire — generally the last of the charcoals. More hot charcoals were spread on top of the lid.

In today's world, this *dum* method of cooking is the equivalent of slow oven baking. The aromatic *garam masala* is sprinkled over the top before the pot is sealed again. When the lid is finally removed, the enticing aromas of the meat mixed with the *garam masala* fills the room.

If you like, leave out the cayenne in this recipe — that is probably what the early Moghuls did. The later Moghuls, seduced by the chili peppers brought from the New World by the Portuguese, used it generously.

Any of the rice dishes in this book, particularly Rice and Peas with *Garam Masala* (page 65), would be a wonderful accompaniment.

You could also make this dish with stewing lamb from the shoulder. In that case, the baking time would be less, about 1 hour and 5 minutes.

SERVES 4 TO 6

10 small turnips, about 1 1/2 pounds without leaves and stems, peeled (larger turnips should be halved)

2 3/4 teaspoons salt

6 tablespoons vegetable oil

2 pounds boneless stewing beef from the neck and shoulder, cut into 1 1/2 inch cubes

3 medium onions, peeled and minced

6 garlic cloves, peeled and minced

1 tablespoon ground coriander

1/8 – 1/2 teaspoon cayenne pepper

1/2 teaspoon very coarsely ground black pepper

1 1/4 cups plain yogurt, beaten lightly

1 teaspoon ground garam masala *(page 20)*

Prick the turnips all over with a fork. Put them in a bowl and rub them with 3/4 teaspoon of the salt. Set aside for 1 1/2 to 2 hours.

Preheat the oven to 350° F.

Heat the oil in a wide, flameproof casserole over medium-high heat. When hot, put in as many meat pieces as the pot will hold easily in a single layer. Brown the meat on all sides and set aside on a deep plate. Brown all the meat this way, then set aside.

Add the onions and garlic to the pot and turn the heat down to medium. Stir-fry the onion-garlic mixture for about 10 minutes, or until it has browned. Now add the browned meat as well as any juices that might have accumulated on the plate. Also add the coriander, cayenne, the remaining 2 teaspoons salt, and the pepper. Stir for 1 minute. Now add the turnips, yogurt, and 1 cup water. Stir and bring to a brisk simmer over medium-low heat. Simmer briskly, uncovered, for 5 minutes, stirring now and then. Sprinkle *garam masala* over the top and stir to mix. Cover tightly, first with aluminum foil and then with a lid, and bake in the oven for 1 1/2 hours. On a medium-high flame, reduce liquid so it clings to the meat and turnips, turning gently now and then. Spoon off the oil that floats to the top before serving.

BARBECUED LEG OF LAMB WITH A SPICY, LEMONY MARINADE

Sainki Hui Raan

A spectacular summer feast prepared outdoors on the barbecue, this is really an all-season dish that can easily be broiled indoors during the rest of the year.

It consists of a leg of lamb that has been butterflied, or boned so that the whole piece lies flat, rather like a large, slightly uneven steak. It is then marinated in a paste that includes lemon juice, the "wet" trinity — onions, garlic, and ginger — the "dry" trinity — coriander, cumin, and turmeric — as well as the aromatic *garam masala* and cayenne pepper. To get the paste to flavor the meat all the way through, cut deep slits into the flesh and marinate for 24 hours or longer.

Unless you can get a 4- or 5-pound leg, ask your butcher to butterfly a whole 8- to 9-pound leg of lamb and remove *all* the skin and fat on the outside. Cut the meat in half and freeze one half for future use, unless you are entertaining a large group, in which case the recipe can easily be doubled.

Serve with Browned Cabbage with Fennel and Onions (page 42) or Eggplant Baked in a Sweet-and-Sour Tamarind Sauce (page 46) and any rice dish. You may also serve this with plain rice and a salad. In the summer, it is just perfect with sliced tomatoes, Cucumber Wedges with Roasted Cumin-Coriander Powder (page 106), corn on the cob, and boiled potatoes rubbed with oil and grilled along with the meat.

SERVES 5 TO 6

1 small onion, peeled and coarsely chopped

A piece of ginger 1 1/2 inches long and 1 inch wide, peeled and coarsely chopped

2 – 3 garlic cloves, peeled and coarsely chopped

1/3 cup lemon juice

1 1/2 teaspoons ground coriander

1/2 teaspoon ground cumin

1 teaspoon ground garam masala (page 20)

1/2 teaspoon turmeric

3 tablespoons olive oil

1 1/4 teaspoons salt

1/2 teaspoon freshly ground pepper

1/4 – 1/2 teaspoon cayenne pepper

Half an 8- or 9-pound leg of lamb, boned and butterflied

Put the onion, ginger, garlic, and 2 tablespoons of the lemon juice in a blender, and blend at high speed until you have a smooth paste (if more liquid is needed, add more lemon juice).

In a nonmetallic bowl large enough to hold the meat, put the paste from the blender and all other ingredients except the meat. Mix well.

Carefully cut off all fat and tissue from the meat, and with the point of a knife, make lots of jabs in it on both sides. Put the meat in the marinade paste. Make a few more jabs with the knife, being sure the paste gets rubbed into the meat and goes way inside the gashes. Cover the container and leave refrigerated for 24 hours. Turn the meat over at least 3 or 4 times during this period.

The meat is now ready for grilling. Light your fire. If it takes 20 to 30 minutes to get red-hot, start about 1 hour and 15 minutes before you intend to eat. When hot, place the metal grill on the lowest notch.

Lift the meat out of the bowl, leaving marinade, and place on the grill. Sear 5 to 8 minutes (depending on your grill) on either side. Now raise the grill to its topmost notch and cook about 20 minutes on each side, brushing the side facing the coals frequently with the marinade until it is used up. If you don't have a grill that moves up and down, just remember that the meat needs to cook about 50 minutes and it should be very dark on the outside and pinkish inside. If you have a globe-shaped grill, cover during this part of the grilling. Most Indians like their meat well done; you may prefer it a bit rare, but don't cook it too rare, as the spices inside won't get a chance to cook through.

Place the meat on a carving board and let rest for 15 minutes. Cut it as you would a flank steak, into thin slices with the knife held at a slight angle to the board.

Black Pepper

RELISHES AND CHUTNEYS

YOGURT RAITA WITH TOMATO AND CUCUMBER

Timatar Aur Kheeray Ka Raita

A cooling delight, perfect for hot, spicy meals or for eating by itself. The main seasoning for the *raita* is the musky, aromatic roasted and ground cumin seed. Cumin is also meant to be a "cooling" spice. Serve with all Indian meals.

SERVES 4 TO 6

2 cups plain yogurt

1/2- 3/4 teaspoon salt

Freshly ground black pepper

1/8 teaspoon cayenne pepper

1/2 teaspoon ground roasted cumin seeds (page 18)

1 small tomato, cut into small dice

About 4 inches of cucumber with small seeds, peeled and cut into small dice

Put the yogurt in a bowl and beat lightly with a fork until smooth. Add all the remaining ingredients and mix well.

Cumin

YOGURT RAITA WITH
ROASTED CUMIN

Gajar Aur Kishmish Ka Raita

The taste of this *raita* takes me back to the hundreds of festive banquets I have attended where a sweet-and-sour relish of this sort was always served with the main meal. The sweetness comes from the carrots, the sugar, and the raisins, the tartness from the yogurt. The spices include a *tarka* (page 10) of mustard and cumin seeds, which provides a wonderful nuttiness. Notice that the raisins are also allowed to caramelize briefly in the hot oil.

You may serve this at most Indian meals in small, individual bowls, if you like. In that case, a teaspoon would be the best eating implement. At a family meal, it could also be served at the end, as a salad-cum-dessert.

SERVES 4

1 1/4 cups plain yogurt

1/2 teaspoon sugar

1/4 teaspoon salt

1/4 teaspoon cayenne pepper

1 medium carrot, peeled and coarsely grated

1 tablespoon vegetable oil

1/4 teaspoon cumin seeds

1/4 teaspoon brown mustard seeds

2 tablespoons golden raisins

Put the yogurt in a bowl and beat lightly with a fork until smooth and creamy. Add the sugar, salt, cayenne, and carrot. Mix.

Heat the oil in a very small frying pan over medium-high heat. When very hot, add the cumin and mustard seeds. As soon as the mustard seeds begin to pop — this just takes a few seconds — add the raisins. Stir once and quickly empty the contents of the pan, oil and all, over the bowl of yogurt. Mix.

CUCUMBER WEDGES WITH ROASTED CUMIN-CORIANDER POWDER

Kheeray Ke Tukray

These deliciously crunchy wedges of spiced cucumber are seasoned with a very Gujarati mixture — coriander and cumin seeds that have been roasted and ground together. You will have to make more than you actually need of this mixture in order to grind it properly, but whatever is not used may be stored in a tightly covered jar for future use.

Serve with any Indian meal. It is best to prepare this at the last minute, just before you sit down to eat. I have a preference for Kirby or pickling cucumbers, but you may use whatever kind you prefer.

SERVES 4

> 2 medium cucumbers or 4 kirbies
> Juice of 3/4 lemon
> 1/4 teaspoon salt
> 1/8 teaspoon cayenne pepper
> Freshly ground black pepper
> 1/2 teaspoon ground roasted cumin and coriander seeds
> (page 18)

Peel the cucumbers and cut them in half crosswise, then cut each half into 4 sections lengthwise. Arrange the wedges on a serving plate in a single layer. Squeeze the lemon juice over the top. Sprinkle the salt, cayenne, black pepper, and cumin-coriander mixture over them evenly. Serve immediately.

RED PEPPER CHUTNEY WITH MINT AND ALMONDS

Lal Chutney

This is the chutney traditionally served with the Peshawari Kebabs on page 96. I now like it so much I serve it with many of my meals. The seasonings are mostly fresh ones — fresh mint, fresh dill, and lemon juice.

Instead of fresh long hot red chilies, which are often hard to find, I have used a combination of fresh red bell pepper and cayenne pepper. You may use just the fresh chilies, if you so wish — and if you can find them — and the chutney will be much hotter. Also, walnuts may be used instead of the almonds. Both are traditional and authentic.

This chutney may be kept in the refrigerator for a few days.

SERVES 8

1/2 large red bell pepper, seeded and coarsely chopped
20 large fresh mint leaves or 30 smaller ones, coarsely chopped
2 tablespoons lemon juice
1 garlic clove, peeled and coarsely chopped
1/2 teaspoon cayenne pepper
1/2 teaspoon salt
Freshly ground black pepper
1 tablespoon chopped slivered blanched almonds
1 teaspoon chopped fresh dill

Put the red pepper, mint, lemon juice, garlic, cayenne, salt, and black pepper into a blender in the order listed and blend until smooth. Add the almonds and blend again. A few bits of almond may be left unpulverized. Pour into a bowl and check for seasonings. Mix in the dill.

TAMARIND CHUTNEY WITH BANANAS AND RAISINS
Imli Ki Meethi Chutney

With recipes for Tamarind Paste and Tamarind Chutney

In this family recipe, the chief flavor for the sweet-and-sour chutney is provided by roasted and ground cumin seeds. Nothing else is needed. The match of tamarind and roasted cumin was obviously made in heaven!

The basic tamarind paste, without any additions, can be made in advance, as can the basic tamarind chutney, without the addition of raisins and bananas. They last about 2 weeks in the refrigerator and may also be frozen indefinitely. The final, fruit-filled chutney can be served with most Indian meals except those using the paste or basic chutney in a recipe.

SERVES 4 TO 6

1 piece of tamarind, the size of a large tangerine
6 tablespoons sugar, or to taste
3/4 teaspoon salt
1 1/2 teaspoons roasted ground cumin (page 18)
1/8 – 1/4 teaspoon cayenne pepper (optional)
1 tablespoon golden raisins, soaked in hot water for 2 hours
1 ripe but firm banana, peeled

Break up the tamarind into small pieces and soak them overnight in 2/3 cup hot water in a small nonmetallic bowl or cup so pieces are covered. The next morning, mash the soaked tamarind in the water, making a thick, uneven pulp using your hands or the back of a wooden spoon.

Place a strainer over a nonmetallic or stainless steel bowl. Put the tamarind pulp in the strainer, and press down with the back of a wooden spoon. Keep pressing until nothing but fibrous tissues and seeds are left in the strainer. Put the fibrous tissues and seeds in a clean bowl and add another 2 tablespoons of hot water. Mash some more. Put back in strainer and strain some more. Discard fibrous tissues and seeds. Make sure you scrape off and keep all the strained pulp on the outside of the strainer — it doesn't always drip down. (This is the basic tamarind paste used in the pork recipe, page 90. It may be frozen.)

Mix the strained pulp with the sugar, salt, cumin, and cayenne, tasting as you go to get a perfect balance of flavors. (This is the basic tamarind chutney used in the eggplant recipe, page 46. It may also be frozen. A couple of tablespoons of this chutney can be spooned over yogurt relishes for an added sweet-and-sour taste.)

Drain the raisins and add them to the chutney. Just before eating, cut the banana into 1/4- to 1/3 -inch thick slices and mix with the tamarind pulp.

T a m a r i n d

SWEET TOMATO CHUTNEY WITH BENGALI FIVE SPICES

Timatar Ki Meethi Chutney

This chutney is flavored with an initial *tarka* (page 10) of the Bengali five-spice mixture *panchphoran*, but it is the aniselike taste of fennel that seems to linger most. It is important that you have all the spices ready and at hand before you start cooking, since they go into the pot in quick succession and should not be allowed to burn.

If you wish to make this chutney with fresh tomatoes, use red-ripe ones when they are in season. To peel them, drop them into boiling vinegar for 10 to 15 seconds, then lift them out and peel.

When cooked and cooled, this chutney should be sweet, sour, and thick as honey. It may be served with all Indian meals and Western ones as well.

MAKES ABOUT 2 1/2 CUPS

6 garlic cloves, peeled and coarsely chopped

A 2-inch piece of fresh ginger, peeled and coarsely chopped

1 1/2 cups red wine vinegar

3 tablespoons mustard oil or extra-virgin olive oil

1/4 teaspoon brown mustard seeds

6 fenugreek seeds

1/4 teaspoon cumin seeds

1/4 teaspoon fennel seeds

1/8 teaspoon kalonji

A 1 3/4-pound can whole tomatoes, or 2 pounds fresh tomatoes, peeled and seeded

1 1/2 cups sugar

1 1/2 teaspoons salt

1/8 – 1/2 teaspoon cayenne pepper, according to taste

3 tablespoons golden raisins

Put the garlic, ginger, and 1/2 cup of the vinegar into a blender and blend at high speed until smooth.

Heat the oil in a medium, noncorrosive heavy-bottomed pot over medium-high heat. When hot, add the mustard seeds. As soon as they start to pop — this takes just a few seconds — add the fenugreek, cumin, fennel, and *kalonji*. Stir once quickly and add the paste from the blender. Stir the paste for 1 minute and add the tomatoes and juice from the can, the rest of the vinegar, and the sugar, salt, and cayenne pepper. Bring to a boil. Lower heat a bit and cook, uncovered, over medium heat at first and then, as the chutney thickens, on increasingly lower heat for about 1 1/2 to 2 hours, or until chutney becomes thick. A film should cling to a spoon dipped in it. Stir occasionally at first and more frequently as it thickens. You should end up with about 2 1/2 cups of chutney. Add the raisins. Simmer, stirring, another 5 minutes. Turn heat off and allow to cool. Pour the chutney into bottles or jars. Keep refrigerated.

Kalonji

ONION SLICES WITH MINT AND CAYENNE

Pyazka Laccha

Just as almost no meal in India is served without chutneys and/or pickles, no meal is served without something raw. This could take the form of sliced tomatoes, thinly sliced red onions, pencil-thin cucumbers, raw slices of kohlrabi, radishes or scallion. These are just munched along with the meal, sometimes plain, sometimes dipped in a mixture of salt, pepper and ground, roasted cumin. Sometimes, many of these same vegetables are combined and lightly dressed with the dressing varying considerably, depending upon the part of India you are from.

Our family in Delhi, had *laccha* on the table at every meal. This consisted of very finely sliced onion rings or half-rings, dressed, at their simplest, with some salt, pepper, cayenne and lemon juice. Tomatoes and fresh mint were frequently added. Here is our family recipe:

SERVES 4

3/4 cup very thinly sliced onion half-rings

1 plum tomato (or other small tomato) cut into fine rounds

1/4 teaspoon salt

Freshly ground black pepper

A generous dash of cayenne pepper

1 teaspoon white vinegar or lemon juice

A few leaves fresh mint, chopped

Combine all ingredients and mix gently. Taste for balance of salt, sour and hot, adding more seasonings as needed.

DESSERTS AND DRINKS

CARROT CAKE WITH PISTACHIOS

Gajar Ki Cake

All sorts of Western confections are made in India, many of them with somewhat Indian flavors. Here, instead of the usual vanilla, cardamom is used. For all Indian desserts, cardamom is our vanilla. Take the seeds out of the pods and grind them very finely in a mortar. (Larger quantities of seeds may be ground in a clean coffee grinder.)

Serve with Spiced Tea with Cardamom and Cloves (page 119) or with Cucumber Lemonade with Ginger (page 118).

SERVES 6 TO 8

2 teaspoons plus 4 tablespoons butter, softened

1 cup unbleached all-purpose flour, plus extra for dusting

1 teaspoon baking soda

1/4 teaspoon salt

2 large eggs

1/2 teaspoon ground cardamom

1 cup sugar

1 1/2 cups peeled and grated carrots, well packed

2 tablespoons chopped pistachios

2 tablespoons chopped walnuts

2 tablespoons golden raisins

Rub a 9-inch round nonstick cake pan that is 1 1/2 inches in height with the 2 teaspoons butter and then dust very lightly with flour.

Preheat the oven to 350° F.

Sift 1 cup flour with the baking soda and salt.

Beat the eggs well in a large bowl. Add the cardamom, sugar, and 4 tablespoons softened butter. Keep beating until all ingredients are thoroughly mixed.

Add the sifted flour mixture to the ingredients in the large bowl and fold in gently with a spatula. Add the carrots, pistachios, walnuts, and raisins. Fold in gently as well.

Pour the cake batter into the cake pan and bake for 35 to 40 minutes, or until a toothpick inserted comes out clean and the top is a golden red.

C a r d a m o m

RICE PUDDING WITH CARDAMOM

Kheer

This delicate rice pudding uses very little rice. It is thickened more by letting the milk boil down to a creamy consistency. The flavoring comes from cardamom and nuts.

Serve this pudding in individual custard bowls, or, if you prefer, put it all in one shallow bowl from which people can serve themselves. It is the perfect dessert to end any Indian meal.

SERVES 4

2 quarts milk

2 tablespoons long-grain rice

9 cardamom pods, slightly crushed

3 tablespoons sugar, or to taste

1 tablespoon slivered pistachios

1 tablespoon slivered blanched almonds

Combine the milk, rice, and cardamom in a wide, heavy-bottomed pot. Bring to a boil, then lower heat to medium so mixture does not boil over. Cook, stirring now and then, until milk is reduced to 4 cups. This may take an hour or more, depending on your pot. Turn off heat.

Remove cardamom pods and discard. Add sugar and most of the nuts. (Save some for garnishing.) Mix well. Leave to cool. Cover and refrigerate. Sprinkle nuts over the top before serving.

SWEET LASSI WITH MANGO
AND CARDAMOM

Aam Ki Lassi

Soothing and satisfying, this can be made with the peeled flesh of
fresh ripe mangoes or with good canned ones. (Drain the canned
mangoes before using.) The only seasoning is cardamom. The
seeds should be taken out of the pods and ground very finely in a
mortar. Serve with a meal or as a midday snack.

SERVES 2 TO 3

1 1/4 cups plain yogurt

1 cup chopped ripe mango pulp

3 tablespoons sugar, or to taste

1/4 teaspoon ground cardamom

8 ice cubes

Combine all ingredients in a blender and blend until almost
smooth. Some ice pieces will remain. Pour into 2 or 3 glasses and
serve.

CUCUMBER LEMONADE
WITH GINGER

Kheeray Aur Nimbu Ka Paani

A cooling drink for a steamy hot day, this lemonade gets most of its liquid from cucumber. It is flavored with fresh ginger. The best way to grate ginger to a pulp is by using a Japanese ginger grater. All Japanese suppliers seem to sell them. Then, to get the juice, simply squeeze the pulp. The smallest holes of an ordinary grater may also be used.

Stick sprigs of fresh mint in the glasses before serving. Serve before a meal or as a thirst quencher.

SERVES 2

2 teaspoons fresh peeled ginger, grated to a fine pulp (see above)
1/2 cup fresh lemon juice
4 1/2 tablespoons extra-fine sugar, or to taste
1 medium cucumber
10 ice cubes

Squeeze the juice from the ginger pulp into the lemon juice. Add the sugar and mix thoroughly. Pour equally into 2 glasses.

Peel the cucumber and cut it in half lengthwise. Remove the seeds. Chop the rest coarsely and throw it into a blender. Blend until smooth. Add the ice cubes and blend until fairly mushy. Pour equal quantities into the 2 glasses with the lemon juice and mix thoroughly. Serve at once.

SPICED TEA WITH CARDAMOM AND CLOVES

Masala Chai

Cardamom and cloves spice up tea most interestingly. They become part of the infusion. Serve with Carrot Cake with Pistachios (page 114), or at the end of a meal, or by itself.

SERVES 4

5 teaspoons black tea leaves, such as Darjeeling
5 cardamom pods, lightly crushed
4 whole cloves

Bring 5 cups of water to a rolling boil. Pour 1 cup water into the teapot, swirl it around, and throw it out. Put the tea leaves, cardamom pods, and cloves into the teapot. Pour the remaining 4 cups boiling water over them. Cover and steep for 4 minutes. Stir and serve plain or with milk and sugar.

SAMPLE MENUS

These menus are offered here only as a suggestion. You should feel free not only to mix and match dishes to please yourself but also to serve Indian dishes with Western ones. For example, broiled or roasted chicken goes well with Spicy, Sour Potatoes with Cumin and Amchoor and with Broccoli with Garlic and Mustard Seeds. Shrimp in a Creamy Aromatic Sauce may be served with any plain rice and a green salad.

A SIMPLE LUNCH OR DINNER FOR A SUMMER DAY

Yogurt Soup with Cumin (page 30)
Ajwain-Flavored Chicken (page 32)
Yellow Rice with Potato and Cumin (page 64)
Spinach with Ginger, Fennel, and Black Cumin (page 54)

A SIMPLE WINTER'S LUNCH OR DINNER

Soothing Cauliflower Soup with Coriander (page 28)
Peshawari Kebabs (page 96) served inside store-bought
pita bread halves
Red Pepper Chutney with Mint and Almonds (page 107)

A MEAL-IN-A-POT FOR SUNDAY LUNCH OR DINNER

A Chicken, Legume, and Vegetable Stew (page 84)
Plain Basmati Rice (page 68)
Yogurt Raita with Tomato and Cucumber (page 104)

A SIMPLE VEGETARIAN LUNCH OR DINNER

Tangy Green Beans with *Ajwain* and Ginger (page 38)
Lentils with Cumin and Asafetida (page 59)
Plain Basmati Rice (page 68)
Yogurt Raita with Roasted Cumin (page 105)

LATE-AFTERNOON OR MID-MORNING SNACK

Spiced Tea with Cardamom and Cloves (page 119) or
Sweet Lassi with Mango and Cardamom (page 117) or
Cucumber Lemonade with Ginger (page 118)
Carrot Cake with Pistachios (page 114)

AN ELEGANT DINNER FOR FAMILY OR FRIENDS

Silken Chicken (page 80)
Rice and Peas with *Garam Marsala* (page 65)
Eggplant Baked in a Sweet-and-Sour Tamarind Sauce (page 46)
Fresh fruit

A LIGHT DINNER

Shrimp in Mustard Seed and Green Chili Sauce (page 70)
Plain Basmati Rice (page 68)
Broccoli with Garlic and Mustard Seeds (page 40)
Fresh fruit

A FAMILY DINNER

Pork in a Tamarind Sauce (page 90)
Browned Cabbage with Fennel and Onions (page 42)
Spicy, Sour Potatoes with Cumin and *Amchoor* (page 50)
Fresh fruit

A GENTLE MEAL

Lamb in a Tomato Sauce (page 94)
Broccoli with Garlic and Mustard Seeds (page 40)
Yogurt Raita with Roasted Cumin (page 104)
Store-bought pita bread

A DINNER FOR FAMILY OR FRIENDS

Whole Fish in Fresh Green Chutney (page 74)
Rice and Peas with *Garam Marsala* (page 65)
Stir-Fried Cauliflower with Ginger (page 44)
Fresh fruit

A TRADITIONAL MEAL

Delectable Pork in Mustard Spice Mix (page 88)
Bazaar Potatoes (page 52)
Stir-Fried Cauliflower with Ginger (page 44)
Yogurt Raita with Roasted Cumin (page 104)
Griddle Breads with *Ajwain* and Black Pepper (page 66)

A WEEKEND DINNER

Shrimp in a Creamy Aromatic Sauce (page 72)
Eggplant Baked in a Sweet-and-Sour Tamarind Sauce (page 46)
Yellow Rice with Potato and Cumin (page 64)
Cucumber Wedges with Roasted Cumin-Coriander
Powder (page 106)
Carrot Cake with Pistachios (page 114)

A VEGETARIAN DINNER FOR FRIENDS

Green Peas with Whole Cumin and Mustard Seeds (page 48)
Spinach with Ginger, Fennel, and Black Cumin (page 54)
Lentils with Cumin and Asafetida (page 59)
Tomatoes Cooked with Bengali Spices (page 56). Serve in
individual bowls
Yogurt Raita with Roasted Cumin (page 105)
Plain Basmati Rice (page 68)
Fresh fruit

A WINTER DINNER FOR FRIENDS

Beef Baked with Turnips and Black Pepper (page 100)
Carrots with Raisins, *Ajwain* and Mint (page 41)
Lentils with Cumin and Asafetida (page 59)
Rice and Peas with *Garam Marsala* (page 65)
Sweet Tomato Chutney with Bengali Five Spices (page 110)
Spiced Tea with Cardamom and Cloves (page 119)

AN ELEGANT DINNER FOR ENTERTAINING

Spicy Cashews (page 31) or
A Dry Chutney or "Dip" (page 36), with raw vegetables.
Serve with drinks
Salmon Poached with Spinach and Bengali Five-Spice Mixture
(page 76)
Stir-Fried Cauliflower with Ginger (page 44)
Green Peas with Whole Cumin and Mustard Seeds (page 48)
Plain Basmati Rice (page 68)
Cucumber Wedges with Roasted Cumin-Coriander Powder
(page 106)
Carrot Cake with Pistachios (page 114)

ANOTHER ELEGANT DINNER FOR ENTERTAINING

Ajwain-Flavored Chicken (page 32). Serve with drinks
Lamb in an Almond Sauce (page 92)
Rice and Peas with *Garam Marsala* (page 65)
Carrots with Raisins, *Ajwain,* and Mint (page 41)
Sweet Tomato Chutney with Bengali Five Spices (page 110)
Rice Pudding with Cardamom (page 116)

A BARBECUE – PICNIC

Barbecued Leg of Lamb with a Spicy, Lemony Marinade
(page 100)
Chickpeas with Ginger and Cumin (page 62)
Zucchini in a Yogurt Dressing (page 58)
Tangy Green Beans with *Ajwain* and Ginger (page 38)
Sweet Tomato Chutney with Bengali Five Spices (page 110)
Store-bought pita breads

A VEGETARIAN BANQUET

Lima Beans with Tomatoes and Raisins (page 60)
Browned Cabbage with Fennel and Onions (page 42)
Tomatoes Cooked with Bengali Spices (page 56)
Eggplant Baked in a Sweet-and-Sour Tamarind Sauce (page 46)
Yellow Rice with Potato and Cumin (page 64)
Yogurt Raita with Roasted Cumin (page 104)
Carrot Cake with Pistachios (page 114)

A GRAND BUFFET

Whole Fish in Fresh Green Chutney (page 74)
Lamb in an Almond Sauce (page 92)
Browned Cabbage with Fennel and Onions (page 42)
Bazaar Potatoes (page 52)
Rice and Peas with *Garam Marsala* (page 65)
Zucchini in a Yogurt Dressing (page 58)
Tamarind Chutney with Bananas and Raisins (page 108)
Rice Pudding with Cardamom (page 116)
Spiced Tea with Cardamom and Cloves (page 119)

A GRAND VEGETARIAN BUFFET

Chickpeas with Ginger and Cumin (page 62)
Lentils with Cumin and Asafetida (page 59)
Tangy Green Beans with *Ajwain* and Ginger (page 38)
Eggplant Baked in a Sweet-and-Sour Tamarind Sauce (page 46)
Bazaar Potatoes (page 52)
Spinach with Ginger, Fennel, and Black Cumin (page 54)
Zucchini in a Yogurt Dressing (page 58)
Yellow Rice with Potato and Cumin (page 64)
Sweet Tomato Chutney with Bengali Five Spices (page 110)
Rice Pudding with Cardamom (page 116)

INDEX

MAIL-ORDER SOURCES

CALIFORNIA

Culinary Alchemy, Inc.
P.O. Box 393
Palo Alto, CA 94302
(415) 598-9143

mail-order business

CONNECTICUT

India Spice and Gift Shop
3295 Fairfield Avenue
Bridgeport, CT 06605
(203) 384-0666

mail-order business; catalogue available; retail shop at regular hours

MISSOURI

Seema Enterprises
10618 Page Avenue
St. Louis, MI 63132
(314) 423-9990

mail-order business; retail shop at regular hours

NEW YORK

Foods of India
121 Lexington Avenue
New York, NY 10016
(212) 683-4419

mail-order business; retail shop at regular hours